James and the Duck

Tales of the Rhodesian Bush War (1964 - 1980)

THE MEMOIRS OF A PART-TIME TROOPER

Faan Martin

authorHOUSE®

AuthorHouse™ UK Ltd.
500 Avebury Boulevard
Central Milton Keynes, MK9 2BE
www.authorhouse.co.uk
Phone: 08001974150

First published by AuthorHouse 8/27/2007

ISBN: 978-1-4343-1973-9 (sc)

*Printed in the United States of America
Bloomington, Indiana*

This book is printed on acid-free paper.

DEDICATION

To my family for their love. You kept me going
during the dark days after the war.
oooOooo

ACKNOWLEDGEMENTS

With grateful thanks to the following:

Frank Herbst who encouraged me to write and who gave me far more confidence than I deserved.

Mike Fisher for doing a great editing job.

Darren Betts for some wonderful suggestions.

Charlottte Lowe for technical advice.

Jayne Martin for allowing me to test numerous whacky ideas on her.

Trina Lee for cover design

Each person mentioned left their mark or marks on this book and in that respect they are also authors of it.

oooOooo

AUTHORS NOTE

This collection of short stories are all based on the truth. Most of them are my own experiences or those of my comrades who were with me. A few are based on stories told to me by friends and which I believe to be true.

Not every word is true. Obviously there are instances where I have had to use my imagination and experience combined with my limited knowledge of the nature, ways, culture, habits, beliefs and mannerisms of the Shona people and those of other tribes. However to the best of my knowledge, the "core" of every single story in this book is the absolute truth, but the embroidery sometimes isn't.

Most of the people's names used in this book have been changed. In a few cases this has been done to avoid humiliating or embarrassing anyone, but most of the changes have been made to protect those former Rhodesian soldiers who are still living in the country (now Zimbabwe) and the ever-dwindling number who return there periodically to visit family and friends.

oooOooo

CONTENTS

BACKGROUND

Rhodesia is now known as Zimbabwe. It is a land-locked country in southern Africa - much bigger than Britain. Mozambique lies east of the country with Zambia to the north, Botswana to the west and rich and powerful South Africa south. Rhodesia had four provinces - Mashonaland, Matabeleland, Midlands and Manicaland.

Geographically the country consists of lowveld, middleveld and highveld. The two main rivers are the Sabi and the mighty Zambezi which hosts Lake Kariba and the majestic Victoria Falls. The Limpopo River which forms the southern border with South Africa is probably the third most important.

Despite economic sanctions after the declaration of independence in 1965, the country continued to develop at an amazing pace. The wealth was generated mainly by agriculture (in particular tobacco exports to more than 30 countries), mining (gold, chrome, nickel, platinum, copper and other minerals) and manufacturing.

The Rhodesian Bush War was fought between Ian Smith's Rhodesian Security Forces and the terrorist fighters of the Zimbabwe African National Liberation Army (ZANLA) which was Robert Mugabe's Chinese backed army and the Zimbabwe People's Revolutionary Army (ZIPRA), Joshua Nkomo's Russian backed forces.

Not everyone called them terrorists. Those that supported them called them freedom fighters. The Rhodesian soldiers started off calling them charlie tangoes (communist terrorists), later they were known as terrorists or ters, then eventually the term gooks became quite popular. Towards the end of the war they were also called floppies. The term "floppie" originated from Rhodesian soldiers often hearing wounded and dying terrorists flopping around in the dark after having walked into the killing zone of a night ambush.

ZIPRA used the neighbouring country Zambia as a launching pad to infiltrate into Rhodesia. ZANLA used Mozambique after the revolutionary left wing coup in Lisbon, which resulted in Portugal handing their colonies Mozambique and Angola back to the local inhabitants.

ZIPRA recruited mainly from the Matabele tribe while ZANLA used Shona soldiers.

Rhodesian Security Forces on occasion also clashed with FRELIMO troops during raids into Mozambique. FRELIMO being the revolutionary group which eventually after many years of war assumed power in Mozambique.

The Rhodesian Army had a few regular units namely the elite Special Air Services (SAS), the Rhodesian Light Infantry (RLI), several Rhodesian African Rifle (RAR) battalions, an Armoured Car Regiment and an Artillery Regiment.

The RAR were unique in a sense. These battalions consisted of African troops and non-commissioned officers (NCO's) with white officers. The RAR had a proud military heritage having fought in Egypt, Burma and Malaya prior to the civil war in Rhodesia.

In addition, the Rhodesian forces relied heavily on their eight territorial infantry battalions and six independent infantry companies. One of these, which didn't last that long, contained a number of former French Foreign Legion troops. Further support came from the police and police reserve.

Towards the latter part of the war, many foreigners joined the Rhodesia Army. Some of them were American and Australian Vietnam veterans.

Two specialist units, the Selous Scouts and the mounted Grey's Scouts were later formed.

Although tiny and equipped with outdated aircraft the Rhodesian Air Force played a major role in Rhodesian military successes. The aircraft consisted of a handful of Canberra bombers, Hawker Hunter fighter-bombers, Vampire jets and civilian propeller-driven aeroplanes (known as Lynx and Genet) which were converted into military aircraft. In addition there were transport aircraft (Dakotas, Britten-Norman Islanders and Trojans).

The Alouette helicopters played an extremely important role both as transport aircraft and as gunships. Towards the end of the war (1978) Rhodesia acquired a dozen Bell 205 helicopters which had previously belonged to Israel.

Perhaps the war started in July 1964 when the so called Crocodile Gang killed a white Rhodesian in the Melsetter area.

In 1979 about 200 Rhodesian troops, backed by aircraft and armoured cars, attacked a base in Mozambique containing 6 000 terrorists. Half of the Rhodesian assault force attacked the camp while the other half parachuted into stop group ambush positions. Not only were the terrorists heavily armed and well dug in, they were also equipped with many anti-aircraft guns and could call on support from Russian tanks.

The Rhodesians killed 3 000 terrorists and lost only two of their own men.

Battles involving huge numbers were the exception though. Most of the battles were fleeting close-quarter skirmishes involving only a few soldiers. The Rhodesian soldiers despite almost always being heavily outnumbered, won almost every battle.

Despite that, they lost the war.

The main reason why that happened was because South Africa threatened to cut Rhodesia's supply line if the Rhodesians did not go along with Prime Minister John Vorster and the American, Dr Henry Kissinger's plans for Southern Africa. That supply line was Rhodesia's "jugular vein" in view of the fact that the outside world had applied economic sanctions on the country.

In order to survive Rhodesia needed to export and import and also needed equipment, fuel and ammunition to continue the war. Rhodesia was totally dependent on and could not survive without South Africa.

Robert Mugabe took over on 18 April 1980, not after a military victory, but after a victory at the ballot box.

JAMES AND THE DUCK

WE hated our prisoners that first day – all thirteen of them. Our minds were overflowing with vengeance because our friend, Barry Gibson, had been killed in an ambush only days before and our hearts were still full of grief.

Barry had died a cruel death. The drum of petrol he'd been sitting on had exploded and he had run down the road, a ball of flame, before he mercifully collapsed and died. Our Shona driver, Brokek Munadzi was shot in the head and died instantly. Although we hardly knew him, he was still "one of us." A chap that we knew well, Theuns Coetzee, had to have a leg amputated. Cyril Macfarlane was shot in the butt and later recovered.

The fact that three of the ambushing terrorists had been killed wasn't enough vengeance for us and

1

more important, we hadn't been the ones who had killed them.

Maybe it would have been better if our prisoners had put up a fight instead of surrendering so meekly? Perhaps then, we would have grieved without such a thirst for vengeance.

Instead of fetching the prisoners immediately as we had thought they would, the police let us know that they were far too busy and requested that we keep them until they were able to come. Our officer thought there might be an attempt to free the prisoners so he ordered us to pack up and move camp. Consequently we moved from a wonderful shady spot on top of the escarpment to a real mongrel of a place right down on the Zambezi Valley floor. It was as hot as hell down there. So hot that a bookie who knew the valley well, would have given better odds on heat fatigue killing us than the terrorists.

Rhodesian army officers appeared to have an absolute talent for finding the worst places to base up. The new camp had hardly any shade and when the wind blew, the powdery red dust swirled around the camp and stuck to our perspiration-damp bodies. Neither was there any water nearby so we had to make do with what was in the bowser. That meant no washing apart from a daily crotch and armpits wipe with a wet facecloth.

The duck had come with us.

Our happy little four-man section always made a special effort to have a really good Sunday lunch every week and so my good buddy, Bob Jones, had bought the duck from a friendly old Shona geezer in a remote kraal one afternoon when we were on patrol. As ducks go he was a good one. Medium-sized, plump and quite tame as well. I don't recall the price, but one can be sure it wasn't much. Bob was a bank manager in civilian life and us farmers all knew how tough they could be when we tried to negotiate a loan to get us through a drought.

Someone suggested cooking the duck with a pineapple and for the remainder of that long patrol through the rugged Rhodesian bush, which Rhodesians called "the sticks," we searched for a pineapple. It was like looking for a needle in a haystack. The local peasants only planted little patches of corn, cassava, sugarcane, sweet potatoes and the odd pathetic pumpkin or cabbage around their huts so we joked about having "marijuana duck" on the menu instead. Most Shona villages have a well-hidden patch of what they know as *mbanji* in the nearby bush.

When we eventually returned to our base camp, Bob tied the duck like a dog to a *mutiti* tree with a piece of string. The duck soon became known as Donald. Bob provided him with water and *sadza* (a stiff corn meal porridge which is the staple diet of the Shona and Matabele people). We called *mutiti* trees "Lucky bean" trees, but somehow I didn't think Donald was going to be lucky no matter how many of those pretty little red and black bead-like seeds lay scattered around him. We had been living off tinned food for far too long.

Our plan was to have the duck for Sunday lunch in the base camp, but whenever Sunday came around we weren't there. At dawn on the first Sunday, we were hastily flown by chopper and dropped at a remote village to track a gang of terrorists who had murdered the old headman the previous evening. We tracked them all day until eventually we lost the tracks where a huge herd of cattle had been stampeded backwards and forwards across the trail. The following Sunday we rushed off and captured our current prisoners after receiving useful intelligence from the Police's Special Branch man in the area.

We couldn't wait for the next Sunday to arrive.

At the new camp, we erected a razor wire enclosure for the prisoners in the blazing sun and took turns to guard them at night. During the day we made them dig trenches just in case of a mortar bomb attack. We knew that having enemy prisoners with us would not stop such an attack. In fact we thought it increased the chances of being hit.

Dead men don't talk.

A middle aged, slightly balding prisoner called James was allocated to Bob and I. We hated him that first day and threatened to kick his butt whenever he slowed down with the pick or shovel. Barry's horrific death was still fresh in our minds. I sat there on a pile of earth watching James sweat and thought of Barry's wife Alison. I knew she was pregnant, Barry had told me over a couple of beers the night before he died. I also thought of their tiny son...

Bitter-sweet memories of half-forgotten rugby matches kept mulling around in my head. I recalled playing for my club and for the Manicaland under 20 team with Barry. He had been rather a wild lad – a man's man - who enjoyed life and who was fun to be around.

Despite our many curses and threats of violence, our prisoner-of-war didn't complain at all. He didn't even appear to sulk like the others, but just kept digging away as hard as he could. In no time he had dug our trench and we were about to tell him he could stop when we realised he had other plans. He dug and dug and our trench got bigger and bigger and then he started "fine tuning" the hole in the ground.

It was far bigger and neater than any trench I had ever seen before or since. He dug what can only be described as a huge sunken lounge. It wasn't what American troops call a foxhole, it was a whalehole.

He even dug little "cupboards" for us into the walls of the trench. We later packed our shrapnel and

5

white phosphorous grenades into one of them and our tinned food into another. It didn't end there either, the prisoner insisted on dragging a heavy log and rolling some granite boulders into the pit. He felt we needed some "chairs" to sit on and he made sure there were a couple of extra seats just in case we received guests.

That man thought of everything. Perhaps it was to keep his mind off the predicament he was in? After all, he was facing a highly likely death-by-hanging sentence.

Our family size trench was the envy of the entire platoon and because it was so colossal, our pals joined us in it for a drink that night. James spent the night in the enclosure far away and when we fetched him the next morning to come and tidy up, he was quite amazed to find so many empty beer bottles lying in that hole in the ground. He probably thought Bob and I were responsible for all of them.

The trouble was that we didn't have much to do in that exceedingly miserable camp. We were so bored that we started chatting to our prisoner. It started off with us mocking him, but as the days dragged by and we learnt more about him, the mocking gradually became less and less until eventually it ended.

We discovered he had worked as a cook for an upper class family in Salisbury for many years before retiring in the native reserve. He had a wife and seven kids and also owned a dog, two cows, several goats and some chickens. He even had a bicycle. The bike, he explained, had been given to him as a going away gift by "the master" he had worked for in Salisbury.

By reserve standards he was quite a wealthy man, especially in view of the fact that four of his children were females which he would soon be able to get "*lobola*" for. *Lobola* being a bride price or dowry which in those days was paid in cattle or the equivalent in cash. Something like 10 cows for a desirable woman and maybe one cow for someone not in their first bloom.

Of course an African's idea of "desirable" differs somewhat from that of say an American or European. To an African big and strong is beautiful. Someone built like a Sherman tank can carry huge bundles of wood or a heavy clay jar of water.

African men still pay *lobola* for their wives, but the system is slowly changing. These days many wealthy Africans buy their brides with credit cards. Some African kings have more than a hundred wives and I once met a friendly peasant villager near Chisumbanje in the Rhodesian lowveld who had seventeen.

I recall asking him if he had any regrets about marrying so many women.

"Not really, it's great, but there is one problem," he said. "If I buy one of my wives a new dress the others are furious and cause trouble and I can't afford to buy seventeen dresses at a time."

James told us that he was enjoying his retirement and spent much of his time fishing in the Mazoe River nearby. He confessed that he didn't do much work. His three boys tended to the cattle and goats and the wife and daughters worked in the fields and fetched the wood and water.

"That is so typical of reserve men," Bob said to me.

"They build round huts for a reason - the men crawl out in the morning and sit by the door in the shade with their backs resting against the hut. They move with the shade around the hut until it is evening when they find themselves back at the door and ready to go into their huts again."

Of course he was only joking, but there was an element of truth in the joke. In the tribal trust lands and native reserves it seemed the women did most of the hard work. Conversely the men who worked on the commercial farms worked very hard.

We learnt that James had a great sense of humour, was polite and had led an interesting life. Under different circumstances I'm sure we would have taken to him immediately, but he was one of Robert Mugabe's ZANLA guerrillas. An enemy.

Of course we did ask him the million dollar question, "Why did you become a terrorist?"

His answer, and we noticed he was careful not to let the other prisoners hear him, was that he simply had no choice. He was press ganged into becoming one. It was either join them or die.

Of course he could have been lying...

At night all the prisoners went into their "cage" and then in the morning we would fetch them again to do whatever work there was to do. After the trenches had been completed there wasn't much to do, but we did make them dig a rubbish pit and James was ordered to dig a latrine pit. Again, James proved to outdo the other prisoners. "Just a hole" wasn't good enough for him.

We followed him with our weapons as he examined the surroundings outside the perimeter of the camp for the best site and it didn't take him long to find it either. He picked a tree that had a low and quite thick branch which grew horizontally. He then asked for an axe and chopped the end of the branch off leaving only a huge V sticking out before trimming the smaller side branches off neatly. Then he dug a deep square hole directly beneath it.

When the guys tried his toilet out, they were so impressed they joked that James should patent it. Bob and I felt proud because by then we sort of felt James "belonged" to us.

One morning we ordered James to wash our fire-burnt black pot. We handed it to him greasy as hell and expected him to wash it like we always did. Instead he not only managed to remove the grease, but scrubbed the pot with coarse sand until it looked brand new. The pot had been black for so long we didn't recognise it at first when he handed it back shining like silver.

As the days went by we softened more and more in our attitude towards James. He was fast becoming a friend, but he wasn't one yet. Whenever we handed him the axe, pick or spade Bob and I slipped the safety catches off our automatic FN rifles just in case he thought the tool was meant for one of us.

Eventually Sunday came around again and early that morning three of us started making elaborate plans for lunch. We decided that because none of us were really known for our cooking ability, James should kill, pluck and cook Donald. After all he was an experienced chef.

Bob didn't join in with all the mouth-watering talk about duck for lunch. Instead he turned against us and appointed himself Donald's lawyer. He pleaded with us to spare Donald's life and make a great sacrifice by eating yet another tin of corned beef instead.

He explained that he had become very fond of the duck and wanted to take him home. He concluded his legal argument with a very sneaky, "My kids' dog died recently and I want to give Donald to them as a replacement pet."

After listening to the duck's lawyer, I thought he should have pursued a career in the legal profession rather than the bank. We considered his emotional plea and then decided because we were a democratic four-man section and because Bob had paid for the duck, the fair thing to do was to put the issue to the vote.

Donald was condemned to death. Three votes to one.

The "Duck a la James" was truly superb. I recall that he cooked the duck with a packet of tomato soup.

Bob, of all people, ate more than his fair share which just goes to show that one should never trust a lawyer. Least of all a duck's lawyer.

That wonderful meal in the bush was the straw which broke the camel's back. In our eyes James was no longer an enemy, he was a friend. They say the way to a man's heart is through his stomach.

The next morning the Police arrived to collect our prisoners.

I still recall my sincere parting words to James as I shook his hand for the last time, "James, I really hope they don't hang you."

I heard someone else say, "Now don't lose my telephone number and remember if they don't string you up, I have a good job waiting for you. Just give me a ring when you are free and I'll come and fetch you."

Now why hadn't I thought of that?

Shame the poor old guy was a bit overwhelmed because we made such a fuss of bidding him farewell. He grinned, but I noticed his eyes were watery. The cops couldn't believe their eyes when they saw us all shaking hands with this terrorist, slapping him on the back and wishing him all the best.

Of course they didn't understand....they lived on fresh rations and had not tasted that duck or sat on the Rolls Royce toilet seat invented by James.

oooOooo

ACCEPTANCE AND DESPERATION

The duck and James only came into my life many years later. It all started for me when I was called up for national service. That meant four and a half months of training at Llewellyn Barracks near Bulawayo followed by four and a half months of duty on the border or elsewhere.

The army sent me a train ticket to travel from my nearest railway station to Heany siding near Bulawayo and even closer to the training camp known as Llewellyn Barracks. There were only three of us who came from Manicaland, but as we travelled further west, more and more youngsters joined us. Close to a hundred guys boarded the train in Salisbury that evening and so did a number of military policemen (MP's) who no doubt expected us to cause trouble.

Bottles of all descriptions soon made their appearance and we spent the night drinking and trading stories of what was likely to happen to us during the coming months. One or two guys were warned by the MP's, but I don't think anyone was actually arrested.

At dawn the following morning the train stopped at Heany siding and we were wrenched from peaceful sleep by an irate Sergeant-Major yelling. He was cursing and threatening us in an effort to get us out of our beds and onto the waiting army trucks. He didn't look or sound like someone you could take a chance with so we all got onto the back of the Bedford trucks as soon as we could.

When we arrived at Llewellyn Barracks we were taken for breakfast and I was surprised because the food wasn't only plentiful it was delicious too.

After breakfast we were taken into a hall where we had to write IQ tests. I must have done fairly well because I was told I would be leaving for Gwelo the next day to do an officers' course. However, I politely told the Major I didn't want to be an officer. My older rugby-playing friends who had already done their national service had warned me against becoming an officer.

The Major looked at me in pity as though I was a moron and said, "Are you sure?"

"Yes Sir."

"Okay, it's your decision – live with it."

The next thing I remember was the fastest haircut I ever had followed by my civilian clothing disappearing like mist at dawn. The next time I saw my stuff was nine months later.

I found myself standing in my underpants in a long queue inside a huge aircraft hangar and the next minute a dentist glanced into my mouth and then ordered me to move on to the doctor. The medical man asked me a question or two I think and then stuck his hand under my nuts and ordered me to cough. I obeyed and he shouted "A-one fit" and I moved on again while a scrawny clerk wrote my particulars down.

Then a wise guy behind a counter glanced in my direction and started throwing all sorts of things my way. Blankets, sheets, pillow cases, shirts, shorts, khaki trousers, puttees, anklets, green underpants, green PT vests, boots, sneakers, shoes, more boots, a combat jacket, a hat, a beret, a camouflage cap, a camouflage net and even a sewing kit.

I staggered off towards our barrack room somewhere under the load wondering if any of the clothes or footwear would fit me? Amazingly everything was my size.

That first evening I noticed some of the rookies were keener than others. The keen guys ironed their boots and then started to bone them with polish and water. They also started polishing their brass buckles. The rest of us soon find ourselves a batman and paid him to do the necessary with the boots, buckles and other shiny bits. One wasn't really supposed to employ anyone, but the instructors seemed to turn a blind eye to this practice because I don't recall anyone ever getting into trouble for it.

We spent the next few weeks marching by day and polishing by night. I don't recall sleeping very much. I remember instructors shouting at us day and night. Some of them were scary men.

Some guys just couldn't handle the seven week first training phase. It was tough, but we had many laughs which, at least for me, served to tip the scales back towards sanity. For the first couple of weeks the army put an enormous amount of pressure on us. I'm sure they did that to all new raw recruits in order to instil strict discipline, but at the time we sort of felt like we were being picked on.

After seven weeks we had our first Colonel's inspection and the army made sure that we knew we would receive a pass after the inspection.

We polished all night. We even unscrewed the light bulbs and polished the brass bases. By the next morning the place was immaculate and so were we. We stood there next to our beds not moving and without our trousers on waiting for the colonel to arrive. We didn't move because we didn't want to scratch the polish on the floor and we didn't put our starched trousers on just in case we creased them before the colonel arrived.

When we saw the Colonel's car arrive we started getting dressed and by the time he walked into our barrack room we were ready. The Sergeant-Major shouted "Ten-shun" and we slammed our right boots down as one man and stood there silently with our eyes to the front. The Colonel walked slowly down the room and back again and then told the Sergeant-Major to fall us in outside with the rest of B Company.

Then he let us have it: "You shower of shit! What do ya think you're playing at? Huh? I've never seen such a shabby, backward stinking bunch of trainees as you before, but we'll make soldiers out of you yet. Even if it kills us – or you," he barked.

Every last man's pass was cancelled. It didn't worry me all that much because I came from the other side of the country. The local Bulawayo boys were devastated though. They couldn't wait to see their girlfriends, friends and family again.

We just did the bare minimum for the second inspection a fortnight later. I recall there was even grass growing through cracks in the barrack room floor!

This time after the inspection the Colonel made us fall in outside and then proceeded to congratulate us on improving so much! That was when I first started understanding the army. I then knew it was just a "bullshit baffles brains" kind of organisation.

I remember that first pass well. A small group of us went to a fancy restaurant in Bulawayo for a meal and then to a not-so-fancy bar.

We had to be back in camp by midnight, but when we wanted to leave we couldn't find Neville Bradford. We eventually found him lying in the gutter and half-dragged, half-carried him to the car.

He was our buddy and we worried about him because we knew we had to sign back in with the regimental police (RP's) at the guardroom by the gate. That meant lining up outside and then marching in individually and coming to a snappy halt in front of the desk behind which sat the policeman.

One then had to shout out your rank, name and number before the man would shove the book towards you so that you could sign yourself in.

Not too difficult really, at least not if one were sober.

None of us were, but we felt we would be able to do the necessary. The question was, "What about Neville?" He appeared to be smashed out of his mind.

Fortunately we had enough time to sort our buddy out before we went in. We tucked Neville's shirt in, slapped the dirt off his clothes as best as we could, straightened his beret, wiped the dust off his boots and gave him a stern lecture.

It went something like this: "Now Nev, just hold your pose for a few minutes. March in smartly and do your thing and then march out and we will get you back to your bed, okay?"

"No problem, don't worry guys," he reassured us.

We then joined the line and watched him march in. He did it really well. Upright, tummy-in, chest out and with his back as stiff as a ramrod, he marched in and then halted right in front of the duty RP's desk, slamming his right boot down like a professional soldier. We were proud of our buddy at that moment because he had exceeded our wildest expectations.

He shouted,"Rifleman Bradford 5079 Staff," then he swayed forward and puked all over the desk in front of him, splattering the regimental policeman.

They dragged him off to a cell.

Ted Whittaker couldn't handle the army at all. He became so desperate to get out that he decided to do something about it. One night in the barrack room he took hold of one of his heavy drill boots and proceeded to methodically smash his ankle with the boot heel. He hit it many times as hard as he could.

He did an excellent job. As far as I know he limped for the rest of his life.

We thought it would be a spell in hospital and then home for Ted and we were envious of him. However the army saw things differently.

The Rhodesian Army reckoned that ankle belonged to them so they charged him with "damaging government property." He spent a long time in hospital and then a long time in the military prison at Brady Barracks.

Brady Barracks was no joke. I'd heard that one had to get into the boxing ring against another inmate every morning. If you were beaten up you were done boxing for the day. If you won, then a national champion boxer who worked there got into the ring with you. So, either way you were beaten up every morning.

Eventually Ted did go home after a dishonourable discharge. By then we were trained soldiers and were having a great time on the southern bank of the Zambezi river and we were no longer envious of him.

ooooOoooo

B VERSUS C

Although the spit and polish nonsense never stopped completely the emphasis did gradually swing from drill and cleaning to weapons. We were issued with British 7.62 mm semi-automatic rifles (SLR's) and we learnt to take them apart and re-assemble them blindfolded. One had to be able to do that within a certain time.

We spent a week at a range having our skill with each weapon tested. There were so many different weapons, the SLR, the Stirling 9 mm sub-machine gun, 12 bore automatic shotguns, Star 9 mm pistols and the 7.62 mm machine gun which we knew as the MAG (em-aye-gee). We also fired a couple of Energa rifle grenades and rocket launchers.

When we arrived back in camp the next intake of troops had arrived and we rather enjoyed that because it meant we were no longer the camp's greenhorns.

One evening some of our B company guys came back from the canteen and told us that a guy from C company had knocked Butch Cockerill out cold with a single punch after an argument. That sort of surprised me because Butch looked and acted like a real tough guy.

Then someone suggested that we shouldn't allow C company men to get away with thumping our buddy and so we started planning our revenge. We were aware that they had a Colonel's inspection scheduled for the next morning and wanted to teach them not to mess with B company guys.

We "attacked" them. That meant rolling open tins of Brasso polishing liquid down their barrack rooms. Getting Brasso stains off a polished cement floor was near impossible. I recall tossing a brick through one of their windows and thinking that the barrack rooms sure were old because the entire window frame disintegrated! We also turned a few beds and lockers upside down and knocked some steel cupboards over.

Most of them weren't there when we attacked, but the few guys who were did retaliate and both sides threw a few punches. Nothing too serious though.

I think we all enjoyed that night, if only because it allowed us to release some of the pressure which had been building up in us since we arrived.

The next morning after breakfast we were told to report to one of the lecture halls because our Major wanted to speak to us.

He was not very popular with his troops. I think it was because he was a bit aloof and also a "whiner." He told us that he knew we had attacked the other company and complained bitterly because we had apparently caused 610 dollars worth of damage (a small fortune during the sixties). He said it as though it was an absolute disgrace. We, on the other hand, felt he should have been proud of his men for not taking any nonsense from another company.

He moaned some more: "I will shortly be asking those men responsible for the damage to stand up. You should take responsibility for what you did, it is only fair to the innocent troops for the guilty to own up....." he whined on and on.

When he eventually asked the guilty guys to stand the entire company of more than 150 men rose.

He looked shocked. It was almost as though he thought he had the misfortune to get an entire company of potential criminals under his command. Thinking back now, he should perhaps have been pleased instead because his men had become united so quickly.

We had to pay for the damage, but it wasn't much because we all shared the cost. We were also punished. The entire company was confined to barracks for a week. It was a pain in the butt because we also had to keep on reporting to the guardroom at various times during the day and night wearing different kit each time.

We were also banned from ever walking at Llewellyn Barracks again. Wherever we went we ran. We became fit and strong running around all over the place with our rifles held in front of us. I didn't mind at all because I knew the rugby season would be starting soon.

ooooOoooo

NORTH OR SOUTH?

Throwing a live hand grenade for the very first time can be a harrowing experience. Its a simple task really if one can conquer your nerves. The fact that you held a deadly grenade in your hand might have made some soldiers nervous, but that wasn't my problem. Our instructors made me nervous.

They had this wonderful ability to conjure up pressure from nowhere. They had it down to a fine art. Instead of instilling confidence in the men, they would dwell on everything that could go wrong and also issue threat after threat. They would say things like, "If you mess up and the grenade doesn't get you, I'll have your guts for garters boy!"

Our Sergeant Major was a popular man. Everyone loved him, but they were also fearful of him. He took no nonsense from anyone. He was in charge of our first live grenade throwing session.

Unlike the other instructors, he didn't issue threats, but simply told us what to do.

"You will come into the grenade shelter one-by-one and stand next to me. Then you will show me your grenade in your throwing hand. When I tell you, you pull the pin out and show it to me. Then and only when I tell you, you throw it towards the target which I will indicate. Do not dive down onto the ground behind the three foot wall immediately after you have thrown the grenade because if you do, I will haul you to your feet again. Only go down when I tell you to."

When my turn came, I went in and did exactly as he told me. I was tempted to hit the deck after I had thrown the grenade, but I didn't. Instead I stood there next to the big man and watched my grenade smoking and then he calmly said, "Okay, hit the deck."

The two of us dived down and about two seconds later the grenade exploded and I could hear shrapnel striking the protective red brick wall in front of us.

Later when Gary Stevenson went in we heard an awful commotion and a great deal of swearing coming from inside the shelter just after the bomb had exploded.

Rifleman Stevenson had done everything correctly until he threw the grenade. He was the academic rather than the sporting type and he threw like a girl that day. The deadly grenade instead of being propelled in a forward direction flew straight up above them!

The Sergeant Major, much later and only after he had calmed down, told us that he had looked up at the grenade in the air above them and didn't know where it was going to land.

North of the wall, or south where they stood?

He studied that bomb above them calmly, then panicked when he realised the grenade might come down and bounce right on the low brick wall directly in front of them. That posed another awful question. Would it bounce forward or back?

Were they supposed to seek cover this side of the wall or should they instead dive over the wall and hit the deck there?

It was a question that had to be answered in less than four and a half seconds.

In the end, the Sergeant Major managed to keep his nerve and waited to see where it came down. It landed just on the other side of the wall and so he slammed Rifleman Stevenson into the dirt and joined him there. Moments later, the grenade exploded only a foot or two away.

That was when the Sergeant Major exploded as well.

oooOooo

SAVED BY STUPIDITY

Towards the end of our basic training our company was sent to do a ten day operation on the Botswana border. Some time before, Rhodesian troops had clashed there with a gang of 80 African National Congress terrorists on their way to South Africa. The entire gang had either been killed or captured. Our task was to ascertain whether there had been any further infiltration into the area since then.

In theory it would not be a difficult task because there was no one living in the area, it was part of the Wankie National Park. So if we found any sign of human activity we would immediately know it was terrorists.

Although we never found the enemy or any sign they had been there, several interesting things happened during those 10 days.

It was a part of the country I hadn't been to before and I enjoyed the scenery because it was so different to what I was used to. I came from the Eastern Highlands, and the massive game reserve was all typical flat Rhodesian lowveld with millions of mopani trees. That, in turn, meant coping with what seemed to be millions of mopani flies. Although they are called flies, they are in reality tiny bees and their honey is quite tasty.

The tiny creatures don't sting, but they tend to drive you crazy because they are continually seeking moisture which means they do their level best to get into your eyes. We smoked cigarette after cigarette, letting the smoke drift around our heads in an effort to try to keep them at bay.

The worst thing you can do is kill one of them. That just results in more of them buzzing around your head. Perhaps killing one releases an odour which attracts the others?

I had come into contact with mopani flies before in the Sabi Valley near where I lived, but the hippo fly attacks were new to me. These larger insects weren't as irritating as the mopani flies, but in a way they were far worse because they could and did sting us. Fortunately we only encountered them along a short stretch of the road towards Tjolotjo where we were headed.

On the first patrol, the Sergeant Major slapped my good mate Neville Bradford because he had left his rifle behind in the bush. Their four had stopped for a rest and when they continued, Neville had strolled off without his weapon. After a mile or two, he realised this and told the fearsome Sergeant Major, who was so furious that he belted Neville.

He was no doubt angry because it meant walking back again to fetch the rifle, but perhaps he was also angry because he and the other instructors had failed to get Neville to appreciate how important it was for a soldier never to be separated from his rifle. Later the Sergeant Major, who was a Second World War veteran, apologised to Neville, but my mate didn't hold a grudge because he knew he had deserved the clout.

Our platoon based around one of the many pans of water in the area. It proved to be an extremely wise move for two reasons. First of all, when we arrived we found several species of water birds swimming there and shot as many as we could for dinner. Then later we really appreciated the pan of water because an extremely vicious tummy bug made its presence felt.

One of the guys would be happily chatting to his pals and then the next moment he would crap himself. The bug nailed one man after another without any warning and I laughed myself silly.

Then the next morning I crawled out of my bivvy, stretched myself and suddenly found "it" was running down my ankles. It was the turn of the others to laugh at me. I just stripped and walked straight into the water only yards away and washed myself and my clothes.

From there we went on several long two-day patrols and then met up again at a pre-arranged spot on the map. We were told that a helicopter would pick us up there and take us back to the main base some 40 miles away.

The chopper flew backwards and forwards collecting four guys each time and when it was almost our turn the chopper arrived again, but the pilot switched the engine off and beckoned to us to move closer. He told us he had only enough fuel for one more trip and then gave us a choice – walk or fly, it's your decision.

Of course, being infantrymen, we were all a bit allergic to walking but there were nine of us and Aloutte helicopters could carry only four men plus the pilot and gunner.

Nevertheless, we all wanted to fly so the pilot and the gunner unscrewed and removed panels from the tail of the aircraft and placed them on the floor inside the cockpit. I was told to make myself comfortable on one side of the tail and I was lucky because two guys had to sit on the other side.

I stuck my small pack between my legs and had my rifle in one hand. I wrapped my other arm around a bar and held on for dear life. Six soldiers squeezed into the cockpit with the pilot and gunner and we took off!

It wasn't as bad as I had anticipated and after a while I relaxed and enjoyed the scenery, which was the tops of the trees because we weren't flying very high. When we landed the pilot told us we had set a world record for the number of passengers in an Alouette. To this day I'm not sure whether that was true or whether he had been kidding us.

You could never tell with the Blue Jobs, they always had some prank going...

One of our other platoons had even more excitement.

In those days we still used Second World War Mills grenades and we had been taught how to strip, clean and test them before re-assembling them. It was a simple task.

All one had to do was unscrew the base plug, remove the detonator and clean the grenade. Then you tested the spring. This was also a simple task. You merely pulled the pin out and then held the grenade against your webbing belt before releasing the lever in your hand.

The reason you held the grenade against your belt was to prevent the firing pin from flying into the surrounding bush where you might not find it again.

The last step was to re-insert the firing pin, the lever and holding pin, then to stick the detonator back in and screw on the base plug.

The strange thing was that although we were told to, none of us ever cleaned our grenades unless it was dropped in a puddle of mud or something like that. It just wasn't necessary because it couldn't get dirty inside as it was all neatly sealed.

Johannes Jacobus Gerhardus van der Merwe had different ideas though. Maybe he was just a better and more disciplined soldier than the rest of us, because he decided he would clean his hand grenade.

He unscrewed the base plug and removed the detonator, thereby making it safe. A hot sweaty palm could still cause the detonator to explode, but that would merely blow off a finger or two, or at least that is what our instructors told us.

Then Johannes Jacobus Gerhardus van der Merwe cleaned his grenade. All well so far...

His mistake came next. He placed the detonator back into the grenade, screwed the base plug back thereby making it a dangerous weapon again and then...

He decided to test the grenade against his webbing belt as he had been taught to do. Not that it was necessary to hold it against his belt because he had replaced the base plug so that firing pin was going nowhere. It was going to ignite the fuse.

My close friend, Clive Reynolds, who told me the story was standing chatting to his buddies some two or three yards away from where Johannes Jacobus Gerhardus van der Merwe was diligently cleaning his Mills grenade.

They heard the "pop" sound of the detonator exploding and immediately glanced down to where Van der Merwe sat on the ground. Our grenades had four and a half second fuses and they saw that the grenade placed on the ground directly in front of Van der Merwe was smoking – a sure sign that the four and a half second countdown had begun!

They ran for their lives. Everyone except Van der Merwe. He just sat there staring at the sinister smoke emerging from his hand grenade.

Clive told me that there was a huge dead tree lying fallen near them and he and his buddies all dived through the air in an effort to get behind the tree before the grenade exploded. They made it. Only just.

As they landed heavily behind that tree they heard the explosion of the grenade.

None of them wanted to look to see the results of the explosion because all of them imagined Johannes Jacobus Gerhardus van der Merwe was mincemeat. They expected to see bits of him hanging from the nearby trees.

Eventually they peeped over the log in front of them and to their astonishment saw Johannes Jacobus Gerhardus van der Merwe still sitting in the same place. He was still in one piece, but no doubt his ears were still ringing furiously from the noise of the explosion.

Directly in front of him there was an untidy circular hole in the ground.

What saved him was his incredible stupidity. Apart from managing to explode his grenade he hadn't screwed the base plug in properly either. He had only screwed it in a few turns and the vicious blast had blown the base plug out and down into the ground instead of sending hundreds of deadly pieces of shrapnel flying all around.

The army realised that Johannes Jacobus Gerhardus van der Merwe would be far more dangerous to the soldiers with him than any enemy could ever be and within an hour he was flown away and we never saw him again.

oooOooo

THE SCHOOL OF INFANTRY

The weeks and months at Llewellyn flew past. Perhaps it was because we were never idle. It was polish and drill and shooting on the range. We attended lectures about the various weapons and we spent many an hour dismantling and re-assembling them. We learnt about radios, flares, grenades, rifle grenades and landmines.

We learnt about different patrol formations and hand signals to remain as quiet as possible. We also practised getting in and out of helicopters. Perhaps the most exciting thing I did was calling in a Hawker Hunter air-strike in the Matopos area. It gave me tremendous satisfaction to see the jet suddenly appear with a tremendous noise and bomb the target in front of us.

Map reading became easy after many lectures and we were soon able to navigate through the bush by day or night using a compass. We had several exercises in the beautiful Matopos area in which we used blanks in mock battles.

The medics also came and lectured us about various things. I recall one lecture quite well. That particular medic taught us what to do if a snake bit someone. After the lecture he asked the troops if they had any questions?

"Uh corporal, what must we do if a black mamba bites someone?"

Without any hesitation, the medic answered," If a black mamba bites anyone, close your eyes and repeat after me, Our Father which art in heaven..."

The instructors woke us during the early hours one morning and told us a train had arrived from South Africa and that they wanted it unloaded before first light.

The entire train was full of weapons and ammunition. It didn't take long to do the work because there were about 500 soldiers involved.

A day later we handed our British SLR rifles in and were issued with brand new FN 7.62 mm fully automatic rifles. We were quite excited about that, it felt a bit like Christmas.

I enjoyed the exercises in the bush far more than being in camp where there seemed to be an officer (to salute) around every corner. We also did regular guard duty which was a pain in the butt. The guard duty itself wasn't that bad, but the next day one was always tired because of the broken sleep.

Pay parades were a laugh. One had to march smartly into the pay office and halt in front of the officer. Then you had to salute and shout your rank, name and army number and in addition you had to shout, "Pay checked and found correct Sir!"

That despite the fact that you hadn't even seen your cash, never mind counted it.

Every Friday, when we were in camp and not in the bush on some exercise, we practised drilling for our passing out parade. The Regimental Sergeant-Major (RSM) a most fearsome fellow, was in charge of those parades. Everyone was terrified of him.

He belted many a soldier over the head with a stick that he always carried.

Friday after Friday we tried really hard to get our passing out drill perfect, but we never could. There was always someone who was out-of-step or who turned the wrong way. When that didn't happen someone would drop his rifle or the RSM would notice a belt buckle that was dirty. Of course things like that lit the RSM's fuse and we would have to run to some tree on the horizon and back with our rifles held above our heads as punishment.

Then the big day finally arrived and for the first time we marched to music provided by the Rhodesian African Rifles (RAR) band. They were an outstanding band and we drilled like the Queen's guard in front of all the parents and girlfriends that came to watch. For the first time we never made a single mistake and our passing out parade was quite complicated.

We marched up and down and turned left and right and we open-order marched and saluted with both our rifles and later finishing with an eyes right salute.

The rifle salute was done so well that the civilians started cheering and clapping. We slapped our rifles with our palms as one man and it must have looked and sounded impressive.

That day I learnt that the RSM could smile as well. He was as pleased as punch with our performance and he told us so.

Now we were trained soldiers and suddenly the instructors' attitude towards us changed. They became friendly for the first time and joined us for drinks in the canteen. It became apparent that they weren't the monsters we had suspected, but were merely doing their duty to make soldiers out of us.

We were now members of 1 Independent Company and our platoon would spend several weeks in

Gwelo at the School of Infantry before switching with the other platoon on the Zambian border.

I think we were all glad to see the last of Llewellyn Barracks.

The School of Infantry in Gwelo was like heaven compared to Llewellyn. Our task there was to act as troops for the officer cadets. We gave them a rough time.

I recall a conventional warfare exercise we did in the bush near Gwelo. The officer cadet in charge of us told Nev Bradford and I where to dig our trench. We tried to dig in that spot, but then realised that it was a clay patch which made digging extremely difficult so we just moved ourselves off to an easy-digging sandy patch.

When the instructor arrived to inspect the trenches he was horrified to find that our trench was nowhere near where it should've been. We didn't get into trouble though, in fact he didn't even speak to us. He blasted the officer cadet in charge.

That night we were supposed to take turns to stay awake and guard, but Nev and I were tired from all the digging so we both just slept. Unfortunately some regular troops who were acting as the "enemy," sneaked up on us and stole both our rifles out of the trench while we snored.

Then they "attacked" us by tossing a thunderflash into our trench (those things make a very loud bang) and firing blanks. We leapt up and reached for our rifles only to discover they had disappeared.

We were a bit annoyed about that so we started throwing hard clods of earth at our attackers and they proved to be far better than firing blanks because they soon fled.

Both Nev and I thought we were in serious trouble because we had allowed our rifles to be stolen. However we didn't get into any trouble at all. Our rifles were returned to us at dawn and not a word was said. At least not to us, the instructor blasted our officer cadet. Apparently he should have checked or sent someone else to check that one of us was always awake during the night.

Then the rugby season started. Colonel Parker who was in charge of the School of Infantry was enthusiastic about the game. He was our captain.

Our first game was an away game against Que Que on a Saturday afternoon and were told that we had a pass from immediately after the game until Sunday midnight. The few guys who didn't play rugby didn't get passes.

It was an enjoyable game until I broke my ankle. I knew I couldn't carry on and left the field, but the army saw things differently. The medic at the side of the field, didn't even bother to take my boot off and examine my ankle. He merely wound wide plaster tightly around my ankle and boot and ordered me to get back onto the field and continue playing.

I did and even managed to score a lucky try. After the game we all had a quick shower and then three of my buddies and I set off in a car for Salisbury. They all lived in Salisbury, but I had plans to go and visit my girlfriend in Rusape much further away.

During the game and in the car my ankle didn't hurt much, but when my buddies dropped me off on the Umtali road so that I could hitch-hike to Rusape I found I couldn't put any weight on the ankle at all. They then took me to the railway station instead and I caught a train to Rusape.

After a great few hours visiting my girlfriend, I had to leave again in an effort to make it back to the camp in time. I managed to get a lift to Salisbury and then I stood on the Gwelo road on one leg hoping someone would stop. The very first car did and the driver was a guy I knew through rugby.

His name was Brian Murphy and I had played against him in the Manicaland versus Mashonaland under 20 match the previous season. He had already been capped for Rhodesia's senior team despite only being 19 years old and many years later was the manager of the Zimbabwean team at the World Cup tournament.

We had a most enjoyable chat while we drove and he dropped me right outside the camp. It was already way past midnight and I was AWOL, but I just climbed over the fence, broken ankle and all, hoping the guard wouldn't spot and shoot me.

The next morning I reported to the sick bay because my ankle was very swollen and quite painful. That proved to be quite a laugh because the military doctor was a woman, but I had to call her "Sir" because she was an officer.

The broken ankle proved to be a blessing in disguise. I spent two lazy weeks lying in Thornhill Air Force Hospital with my leg suspended. Andy Donavan who was also only 19 and already a Rhodesian senior rugby player, lay in the bed next to me. He had also broken an ankle. Some years later he also represented Western Province the South African Currie Cup team.

After leaving hospital I was put on six weeks "light duties." Colonel Parker definitely looked after his rugby players because he told me to paint his office and I had six weeks to do it. I could have done it in two or three days.

Some years later Colonel Parker was killed along with other high ranking officers when the helicopter they were in flew into an electrical power line. It saddened me when I heard that because I was fond of him. I think most of my comrades were as well.

Eventually the time came to move on again and we set off in trucks for the long journey to Wankie.

ooooOoooo

POACHERS

When we arrived at Wankie we were told we would be based there for a few weeks and then move to the border camp at Sidindi Island for the remainder of our national service. Wankie was a remote little coal mining village and I suspect the locals were pleased to have us there because we boosted their economy.

We certainly boosted the local hotels' economy.

During our time there, we spent the days playing football in camp and the nights drinking either at our own canteen or at one of the hotels. At the time the South Africans were also in the area doing border duty and they challenged us to a rugby match on the Wankie Mine Club's field.

All the locals came to watch and it was quite an occasion for the little village. Unfortunately we lost, but we were not disgraced.

The only other thing I remember about Wankie was that one night, one of my friends, who had been hitting the bottle too hard, became aggressive and wanted to fight and he selected me as his opponent. I'd done a bit of boxing and felt I could handle him but our mutual friends stopped us from fighting.

Fortunately.

A few days later he did have a fight against one of the cooks. He looked like a natural born fighter and beat the cook to a pulp closing both his eyes. I had been extremely lucky. He would definitely have beaten me up easily.

Then we moved from Wankie to Sidindi Island on the Zambezi River. It was a wonderful wild place and I think we all thoroughly enjoyed our time there.

Our lieutenant was on leave and was supposed to meet us there, but he broke his arm and never arrived. We were told by radio that our new officer would arrive the next day and that his name was James Woodcock.

One or two of the guys in the platoon who knew him told us he wasn't a bad guy at all and that he was a game ranger in civilian life. To me that was bad news because there were wild animals all over the place there. Wild animals you could eat instead of corned beef, but a game ranger would surely not approve of us shooting them, which was illegal anyway.

Mister Woodcock arrived in a Land Rover the next day. The first thing he did was call us together and introduce himself. Then he said, "I'm a game ranger in civilian life and I'm telling you that you can shoot whatever you like, provided you eat what you shoot."

My kind of officer at last.

It was a marvellous place, I recall the first night I was on guard, with a stray dog called Bones that we had adopted, when a small herd of elephant wandered into our camp. I was a bit worried about standing in the dark only ten yards away from a brute of an elephant which was busy stripping the bark off a tree. But I reasoned that if I left the giant animal alone, he or she would leave me alone as well.

Then Bones started barking at the elephants!

I didn't have a clue how elephants usually reacted to a barking dog, but I knew cattle well and I knew cows, especially those with calves, don't like dogs barking at them. They usually rush towards the pooch in aggressive mode with their horns down!

My guess was the elephants would also be aggressive, especially if there were calves in the herd. Bones and I were about to be trampled.

I really love dogs, but that night I nearly strangled Bones because he refused to shut up. He barked incessantly at the elephants while I trembled. I tried to sneak away from him but he stuck to my heels, barking non-stop. Thankfully those elephants appeared to be stone deaf. They just ignored him.

I was no fisherman, but Johnny Goddard caught plenty every day using a hand line. He was a keen angler and must have thought he was in paradise there next to the mighty Zambezi. He taught us all the tricks.

First you catch a vundu (a giant catfish that can weigh around 70 pounds or more) using blue soap as bait. The soap apparently forms a tiny "cloud" in the water and for some strange reason the vundu find this unusual bait hard to resist.

Then you cut a bit of flesh from the vundu and use that as bait to catch the tigerfish. Tigerfish are great fighters; even a small one will test an angler to the limit. I found they were easy to hook, but extremely difficult to land.

Johnny also taught us how to cook the tigerfish. If I remember correctly, he would first gut them and then sprinkle salt and pepper inside them. Then he would squeeze a few drops of fresh lemon juice and a blob of army margarine into them. Now ready to be cooked, he would pack clay around the fish, and shove them under the hard wood coals of the fire and leave them there for ages. Then he would scratch them out with a stick and break the hard-baked clay. The skin would stick to the clay leaving the flesh of the fish exposed.

Those fish were absolutely scrumptious, but you had to eat them very carefully because of all the bones.

I enjoyed the kudu steaks even more than the fish and we shot plenty of the big antelope, which seemed to be everywhere. We ate fresh kudu meat for breakfast, lunch and supper. We also made mountains of biltong, a special version of what Americans call jerky. Throughout Southern Africa biltong is considered a delicacy. It is meat which has been marinated with salt, pepper, spirit vinegar and spices of choice then dried and cured in the shade. Coriander is a favourite spice.

Our camp was crammed with meat. Biltong hung everywhere. Bones became the best fed mutt on the planet and his coat shone from all the *nyama* (meat) he was eating.

One morning just after the guys had cut up yet another kudu we received a surprise radio message.

It was a short and simple: "The District Commissioner is on his way to visit you and he will be there in about an hour."

Oh boy! We couldn't be caught with all the meat we'd poached.

Our officer didn't panic. He just rounded up all the guys, split us into teams and then allocated each team a different "hiding meat" task. Nick Raftopoulus and I were told to take the freshly slaughtered kudu to the edge of the river, and then help the other guys.

We dragged the skin with the head and intestines on it to the edge of the water and ran back to help move the biltong strips and other meat and hide it deep in the bush. After four or five minutes I was back in the camp to collect my second load and happened to glance at the place where we had left the kudu's remains half-in and half-out of the water.

It was gone!

I couldn't believe that a flatdog (crocodile) had taken it so quickly. I shuddered – we swam right there every day. Mind you, we always posted a guard on the bank when we were in the water because a nine-foot flattie could always be seen basking in the sun on a tiny island opposite the camp. The guard had strict orders to fire a warning shot if the croc moved, but it was never necessary.

Two guys once even swam right across that strongly flowing, crocodile-infested river to the other bank just because they wanted to be able to say, "I've been in Zambia."

First they walked upstream for about a mile before diving in. They reached the other bank roughly half a mile upstream and then arrived back near the camp with the return swim.

There were hundreds of crocodiles in that river. I know because I did a long patrol along the southern bank once and saw them. The majority were small, but there were some huge ones as well.

The District Commissioner arrived and spent some time with us and then left, none the wiser that there were a couple of tons of poached meat hidden nearby.

Finally I was able to wave goodbye to my national service and left for home. I would now be a member of the 4th Infantry Battalion based in my hometown Umtali. At first I was only required to do one two-week camp a year, but that only happened once. Sadly the war escalated to such an extent that we were eventually being called up every six weeks for six weeks at a time. The following are a few of the more memorable adventures.

oooOooo

REAR-VIEW MIRROR NEEDED

I

It was a chilly dark night. Neither the cold nor the dark bothered Jacko though. His mind was far away. He wasn't thinking of lying uncomfortably on the hard ground or of the automatic rifle he was holding. Not even about the little twigs and pebbles under him, which after a few hours felt like logs and boulders. He wasn't even concerned about the mosquito raids on his ears. He was used to the bush life and because of it his mind was firmly focussed on other things. Two of them to be exact.

He was thinking of the "twins." Heather's soft rounded breasts. As he lay there in the dark picturing them in his mind, he grinned.

That was when it happened, he later told me. When he least expected it.

Even the corporal's mind wasn't occupied with the ambush and Pete and Fred were also thinking of other things. The corporal was thinking of three stripes on his arm instead of two and Fred was thinking of Dorothy.

Big muscular Pete was thinking of his neighbour, Jeremy Stanfield and what he was going to do to him when he got home. Jeremy had a reputation as a Casanova and in her letters Susan kept mentioning how often he was visiting her to see if she needed any help on the farm while her husband was away in the army. The mere thought of Stanfield alone with Susan was driving Pete crazy. He could think of nothing else.

The corporal was so proud of himself. Although Jacko had been the one who had found the arms cache concealed on the western bank of the Ruya River, it had been the corporal who had stopped him from removing the weapons. He had quickly realised that the arms belonged to someone who would come to fetch them sooner or later. Probably sooner rather than later because the weapons had not been buried, but merely covered with leaves.

His plan was not to disturb the cache, but to ambush it.

Kennedy Maunda's mind wasn't on the war either. As he trudged along the narrow footpath which winded between the kopjes, careful not to step into an antbear hole, he was thinking of a huge pot of *sadza*. He wasn't thinking about the fairer sex because he had just been with a woman and twenty minutes with her had made him ravenous. Besides, with an AK-47 in his hands he could get any woman whenever he liked. He could pick and choose from all the women in a kraal and no one, not even her husband, could stop him. Unless of course the man had a death wish...

That was what Kennedy liked most about being a freedom fighter.

Sometimes he thought he loved his Russian AK-47 assault rifle more than anything else. It was a magic wand in a way. It could get you whatever you wanted. He hoped his would get him a farm one day when the war ended. That white racist pig George Longwell's farm. The house on it was huge – big enough for many wives and a horde of children.

Of course he could have eaten afterwards, but he had arranged to meet Dumisani down by the river at zero two hundred hours to collect weapons for his new recruits and he didn't want to be late. Dumisani was a man to be feared.

He thought of the incident when Dumisani had forced a burning log in between that woman's legs and he started walking faster. They had both known the woman was innocent, but Dumisani had insisted they make an example of her to strike lasting fear into the hearts of the villagers who were forced to witness the cruel act. The atrocity also struck lasting fear into Kennedy's heart.

When they were near the river, Kennedy stopped his men and they listened to see if they could hear anything unusual, but they only heard frogs croaking and beetles singing so he continued to move forward slowly, with his men following five yards apart in single file as he had taught them.

Suddenly he spotted one of his comrades lying on his stomach just ahead of him on the bank of the river which was the agreed meeting place. The man appeared to be sleeping. Kennedy went right up to him and gently kicked the soles of his boots saying respectfully, "Wake up comrade, we are here." He only spoke in a polite tone of voice because in the dark he wasn't sure who the man was and it could have been Dumisani.

Jacko was thinking of Heather lying naked on their bed with "that look" on her face when someone suddenly kicked his boots from the rear and spoke to him in Shona.

Something then happened to him that had never happened before. Something he would probably have nightmares about for the rest of his life. He found his body had involuntarily slipped out of gear and into neutral.

His mind raced like never before. The realisation struck him that a terrorist had sneaked up behind him and was so close that the man had actually kicked his boots! A terrorist with a loaded AK-47 no doubt but there was absolutely nothing he could do about it because he was paralysed. Fear had severed the link between his mind and body and only his brain was still functioning. He badly needed to part his lips to allow his overwhelming terror to escape in a scream that would pierce the African night like never before....but he couldn't.

He just lay there like a sack of salt.

The corporal, lying a few paces to the right of Jacko was equally stunned when he unexpectedly heard the voice, but he hadn't frozen. His mind was in overdrive and he was trying to press himself into the damp ground under him hoping by some miracle no one would see him. Like Jacko he was also drowning in fear. As he lay there motionless, he could clearly hear the terrifying sound of more men tramping through the bush towards them.

Fred was also traumatised and his reaction was to think of the Bible. The words, "This thing you have feared greatly is upon you," lodged in his mind. Another thing, which he feared almost as much, was also upon him. He felt a sudden warm movement between the cheeks of his buttocks, but he was too frightened to be embarrassed.

Kennedy didn't find it strange that his comrade didn't answer him immediately. He merely thought the man had been sleeping and was struggling to wake up. Maybe he had smoked too much *mbanji* (marijuana) or had had too much beer?

Then he spotted the man's rifle. It didn't look like an AK-47!

He crouched and studied the rifle in the dark and when he realised that it certainly wasn't an AK, he felt a wave of heat move up along his spine. He instantly recognised it as cold naked fear because he had experienced exactly the same feeling that time when he was still a boy herding the cattle in Maranke and the lion had come.

In a voice which sounded like someone else's, he uttered *"Kubani*?" (Who?). At the same time he started to swing his weapon down from his shoulder.

Pete was also stunned when he suddenly heard the voice behind him and to his left. It took him a moment to realise what was happening and shake off the disbelief in his mind and then, still lying on the ground, he lifted and swung the heavy MAG 7,62 mm machine gun around with his muscular arms and tugged hard on the trigger.

Kennedy died a split second before he could shoot Jacko. Two bullets struck him in the chest and a third smashed the bone of his upper arm. The force flung him backwards into the dirt like a discarded piece of litter.

The burly farmer fired four joined 50-round belts into the dark of the night without releasing the trigger and the noise and vibrations from the big gun helped ease his fear. The sustained fire of the MAG caused the remainder of the gang to flee into the night. The more defiant ones fired a few wild parting shots.

Within minutes the battle was over, but Fred, Jacko and the corporal continued to blaze away into the dark with their FNs.

A few days later, on the rifle range in our hometown, an instructor told us, the men who were to replace them in the operational area, "From now on all ambushes will have a man facing the rear – is that clear you miserable bunch of pretend-soldiers?"

"Yes sarge!" we shouted back in unison.

oooOooo

BLOOD IS THICKER THAN WATER

Corporal Angus McEwan was ordered to ambush a well used footpath in the native reserve. The Lieutenant showed him on the map where the path was and that evening the corporal led his three men through the bush towards the ambush site. They located the path easily enough and all that remained was to find a suitable spot. Angus scouted around a bit and noted that not far away the winding path passed between two small kopjes of more or less equal height and size. Whenever possible, he preferred to attack from above because he felt it would be easier to withdraw, using the hill as cover if they encountered too large a gang of terrorists.

On a dark night an ambush would of necessity be a close affair, but on this particular night the full moon was overhead. There wasn't a cloud in the sky so Angus knew he would be able to see the path below them clearly.

He slowly led his tiny band of men up the kopje on his left, trying hard not to make a noise but the dry leaves and twigs cracked under their feet and one of his men stumbled which resulted in a rock rolling noisily down the slope. The four soldiers froze until the rock came to a standstill, then they continued their climb.

Unbeknown to him and his men, at that same moment an enemy group was busy climbing the kopje opposite them to ambush the same path. The chances of that occurring must've been a million to one, but truth is stranger than fiction.

When they reached the crest, Angus looked down at the path and was satisfied that it was indeed a good spot to set an ambush from. He could see the path clearly and there was a bit of cover too in the form of a small anthill and the half-buried boulder. He positioned one man on each side of the boulder with the machine gunner behind the anthill and then scouted around for a place for himself.

All three Angus's troops were already lying down when the ZANLA gang on the hill opposite them opened fire and shattered the tranquillity of the evening.

A shot slammed into Angus and spun him around like a leaf in a whirlwind before he fell heavily to the ground. His mind went numb and as he lay there in the moonlight he felt blood running down his leg. He thought it was strange that there was no pain, but thought that was due to being in a state of shock. He was grateful for that, but it didn't stop the panic in his mind.

As the blood gushed down his leg he screamed, "I'm hit! I'm hit!" It was as though he expected his men to drop their weapons and come to his aid immediately. His mind was racing and he recalled the medic telling him how dangerous thigh wounds were because they bled so badly. It felt as though he was about to bleed to death.

His men heard his cries, but the words didn't really register. They were far too busy trying to win the fire fight with the gooks. There was no time to attend to the section leader. That would have to wait until later – if indeed there was a later.

The booming sounds of the two FN 7,62 mm assault rifles and the MAG machine gun firing in short bursts sounded so superior to the cracking sounds made by the enemy's lighter calibre lone RPD 5,56 mm machine gun and AK-47's that Angus's men felt they had a psychological advantage. But they wondered whether their corporal was dying behind them?

Angus continued to shout, "I'm hit, I've been shot!" as his men fired continuously into the rocks and bush on the top of the kopje opposite them. The

Rhodesians' machine gun dominated the fire-fight. Every 10th round in the belt was a tracer which helped the gunner keep his aim low enough to be effective.

The battle was vicious, but it didn't last long. The three soldiers' accurate fire soon put the fear of God into the terrorists and they melted away into the dark night.

As the sounds of battle died down, Angus found out why he felt no pain despite having been shot. An enemy bullet had hit his water bottle hanging from his belt. The force of it had spun him around and the "blood" that he had felt running down his leg was in fact good, clean drinking water from the leaking tap back at base.

When Angus's section returned to camp the next day and told us what had happened we all had a good laugh and no one laughed louder than Angus himself. He showed us his pierced green plastic water bottle and said he was going to keep it as a war momento.

Many years later I thought about my good friend Angus and it didn't seem right to me that a man who, one could say, had been nudged by the Grim Reaper that night, had survived a dozen years of war and several fire-fights only to die a few short weeks after the war ended.

Due to his passion for hunting and tracking, he had been an outstanding soldier and after the war he had gone to help cull some elephants. The group of hunters had surrounded a family of elephants as they always do when culling. When the shooting started, someone on the far side of the circle had accidentally put a .458 round into Angus instead of a jumbo.

It just goes to show that eating health foods all the time, drinking bottles and bottles of spring water, exercising regularly and not smoking won't make the slightest difference to the time that you are meant to go to the Happy Hunting Ground.

When a bullet has your name on it, you will go, even if it is peace time. Alternatively when the bullet has "water bottle" written on it, you won't – although you might think you are already in the departure lounge when the water trickles down your leg in the dark.

oooOooo

IT'S ALL IN THE SHIRT

Although I can still picture the American's face, I can't remember his name. It might have been Joe so I shall call him that. He wasn't a midget, but he was short. As tough as teak, though and as adventurous as they come. He had flown Huey Cobras during the Vietnam War and when the hostilities ended there, he had joined the Rhodesian Air Force and flew one of our French Alouette helicopters.

When I first met him, we were camped on the banks of the lazy old Sabi River near Chisumbanje. We had received a radio message informing us that a lone chopper would be joining our outfit and the next morning Joe and his technician Bill, who manned the aircraft's Browning .303 machine gun, landed in our camp. They were just in time for breakfast.

I was a sergeant at the time and just the week before, my lieutenant had been arrested for a alcohol problem and I had been "promoted" to "acting platoon commander," which was quite different to the real McCoy. Sergeants had a few perks though. They had their meals with the officers when in base camp and it was nice for a change to be served whilst sitting at a table instead of standing in a long queue for your grub. It was also nice to eat off a china plate and drink from a china cup. No more mess tins and tin mugs for me, at least not while I was in the base camp.

The one thing that hadn't changed was the coffee. As always it was heavily laced with copper sulphate, which we all called "bluestone" and which was supposed to stop us feeling randy. The army must've reasoned that Mother Nature doesn't discriminate between ranks when it comes to lust.

After breakfast we enjoyed a good smoke as usual while the day's activities were fine-tuned. That was when the CO asked the airmen if they would mind dropping some troops off near the border. I was amazed at his polite manner. The Major never asked us to do anything, he always ordered.

Joe readily agreed and then he winked at Bill and said, "Hey Billy Boy, shall we do our party trick today?"

Bill laughed and nodded and then the two of them rose and started taking their shirts off. We wondered what was going on while they exchanged shirts. The Flight Lieutenant now looked like a Colour Sergeant gunner and the Colour Sergeant gunner looked like a pilot.

They composed themselves and then strode towards their aircraft while the waiting troops were called closer. The two airmen and the four troopers clambered into the doorless helicopter. Gunner Bill seated himself behind the controls while his officer sat behind the Browning with its long belt of shiny brass cartridges.

Then when everyone was ready to go, Bill glanced over his shoulder and ever so casually said, "Hey, Joe man, I really don't feel like flying this bird today. You fly it and I'll take the gun."

As his bewildering words sank in, the troopies' eyes went wide. Had they heard right?

Joe and Bill quickly exchanged places and the watching troops' eyes became wider still. Now with Bill and his flight lieutenant pips on his shoulder, sat behind the gun and Joe, with colour sergeant stripes on his arm, behind the aircraft's controls, Joe, sounding rather concerned, said, "Do you think it will be OK sir? You know I haven't flown for years and never this type of helicopter?"

"Don't worry about it Joe, just fly. You'll be fine, you've watched me often enough," Bill answered far too casually for the troops' liking.

As we stood there watching and now realising what was happening, we struggled not to laugh and give the game away. The four soldiers kept glancing at each other with worried enquiring expressions on their faces. No one said a word. Everything had happened too quickly and they were stunned into silence.

Before anyone could complain, Joe started the powerful engine and the rotor blades started to turn, slowly at first but gradually picking up speed until they became a blur. The noise was deafening and the grass beneath and around the chopper was flattened by the downdraft. Now it was too late for the soldiers to protest. No one would hear them.

I studied the faces of my comrades inside the helicopter and to me they looked like rats staring into the eyes of a black mamba. They had that dull, sad and resigned look as though they knew the end had come. There were a few glances in our direction by eyes pleading for help.

Then Joe suddenly made the chopper leap violently into the air which resulted in the troopies grabbing each other. Worse was to follow. Instead of flying off smoothly, Joe made that whirly-bird spin around and around in a circle whilst at the same time swaying from side-to-side like a girl with a hula hoop around her hips. Joe's performance as a pilot who couldn't fly was deserving of an Oscar. By then it was all just too much for us on the ground and we fell about laughing...

Then in an instant, Joe steadied the aircraft, looked our way and winked extravagantly before flying off smoothly towards the border.

oooOooo

MY PAL THE MERCENARY

I met the late Lieutenant George Quarry so many years ago, but I still remember his first words to me. He said, "So this is the African jungle." That struck me as rather strange at the time because we training at the Mazoe Dam not far from Salisbury and it was hardly jungle. Rural yes, grass and trees yes, but it was hardly "Tarzan territory."

The clean cut officer told me he was from New York which didn't impress me. He also told me that he had fought in Vietnam with the Green Berets which did impress. He said he'd been a captain with the crack American unit, but had to drop a rank when he joined the Rhodesian Light Infantry known as the RLI. That was standard practice.

Why had he come to war-torn Rhodesia and taken a job that classed him as a mercenary? It didn't make sense to me. Why would anyone leave one of the most powerful armies on the planet to throw in his lot with little old Rhodesia's hopelessly outnumbered warriors? It certainly couldn't have been for the money? We were poorly paid.

Soon I was sorry I had asked. He explained that his wife had messed around with some other guy while he had been in Vietnam. The whole mess had ended in divorce. After the war in South East Asia had ended, George had felt there wasn't good enough reason for him to continue living in New York and so he decided to rather go and fight against more communists in Rhodesia until his future became clear.

Even that was ironical in a sense because although Mugabe and Nkomo's armies were backed by the Soviet Union and China respectively, there probably wasn't a single true communist in either movement. People who sell their daughters for cows aren't interested in communism.

Lieutenant Quarry's explanation made as much sense to me as a crime of passion makes sense to the French. In the American's case it was a war of passion.

I recall that first night when we sat around a fire smoking and drinking while we traded stories. We soon became firm friends and he wanted to know all about Rhodesia and the war, while I wanted to learn more about the USA and Vietnam. His stories about the Vietcong digging tunnels and living inside hollowed-out mountains intrigued me. I also recall him telling me that during one battle an eavesdropping American warship captain off the coast had come on the air and offered his help. The unseen ship's big guns had pounded the mountain in most impressive fashion George told me.

His words made my thoughts turn to the Rhodesian "Navy." The only navy I knew about was a tiny motor boat on the blue waters of Lake Kariba with a mounted machine gun. I decided not to tell George about this just in case it made him decide to return to the USA pronto. We needed every man we could get.

We spent a week together at the dam which resulted in ever-increasing puzzlement for the New Yorker. I was in the habit of asking Corporal Josiah Maluwa for the time. It was a sort of game we played which only an African would understand. Every now and again I enquired about the time and Josiah always answered promptly. It eventually became too much for George and he confronted me.

"How the hell is Josiah supposed to know the time when he isn't even wearing a damn watch?"

I chuckled and told him that many Africans, who had never owned a watch and couldn't read one anyway, could tell the time by merely looking at the sun's position in the sky.

"They know," I went on, "that when the sun is directly overhead it is noon. Using that as a marker they make a calculated guess at the correct time."

He shook his crew-cut head in disbelief and said, "I would never have believed they could be so accurate, but I've been checking on my watch and Josiah is never more than a couple of minutes out."

It was my turn for disbelief.

I lost contact with George after that, but a few years later, during a battle with a group of 200 insurgents on my own farm, of all places, we almost met up again. While my wife and I were watching the helicopter gunships flying in a circle and taking turns to pound the enemy positions with machine gun and cannon fire, I spotted a Dakota flying in from the west and I thought, "Oh great, paratroopers as well."

I asked a Rhodesia Light Infantry trooper if he knew George Quarry? He chuckled and replied, "You bet I do. In fact, he is in that Dak up there right now."

We continued to chat about George while watching the Fire Force choppers striking at the enemy. Then a Lynx darted in and dropped a green plastic drum of fran-tan into the clump of waterberry trees which my cattle loved to use for shade. I was grateful that I'd moved the herd to another camp just the day before. Fran-tan was vicious stuff. We called it fran-tan, but George had told me that they called it napalm.

The RLI soldier told me that George had married a Rhodesian girl and had adopted her two children from a previous marriage.

"Marriage has changed his life," he added. "That sad-dog look has left his eyes and has been replaced by a happy-as-a-pig-in-mud look. He's a different man now."

It really pleased me to hear that because I too had seen the sadness in George's eyes when we first met.

We watched an Alouette land in the vlei (wetland) before us. A trooper leapt out and placed an orange smoke grenade on the ground before the chopper took to the air again as graceful as a dragon fly.

I knew they were testing the strength and direction of the wind for the paratroopers. I watched the smoke. It seemed incredible that so much bright orange smoke could emerge from such a tiny canister. The smoke left the grenade and promptly did a 90-degree turn courtesy of rather a stiff breeze from the north-west.

No paratroopers jumped that day and sadly I never saw my pal. Not that day nor ever again.

Not long afterwards I read in the *Rhodesian Herald* that George had been killed in action. It made me sad, very sad, because I knew a broken man had rebuilt his life and found happiness again. Now he was gone.

oooOooo

WRONG HAND

There we found ourselves yet again trudging through the dense, but beautiful green Rhodesian bush, loaded like pack mules. This time we were in the Centenary area with me leading and wondering whether I should be scanning the bush ahead for the enemy or looking at the ground in front of me for venomous puffadders? After a while I realised I wasn't thinking of either, I was thinking of her.

We had walked about 45 miles during the previous two days. The walking itself wasn't a problem, it was the weight we carried. Between us we had automatic rifles, bayonets, a machine-gun, plenty of ammunition, both shrapnel and white phosphorous grenades, a claymore mine, wire and detonators, a radio, spare batteries, 32-Z rifle grenades, gas stoves, spare gas cylinders, a medical pack, flares, ponchos, sleeping bags, our rations, cigarettes and whisky: Those precious little bottles were safely rolled up in our sleeping bags.

Two water bottles also hung on our webbing belts. Water is heavy stuff.

Whenever we did external operations into neighbouring Mozambique or Zambia, which was rare, we would leave all the non-essential heavy stuff at the base camp. Tinned food was considered to be non-essential. Instead of tins, a gas stove, mess tins and cutlery we would just take a spoon and a plastic packet filled with a mixture of Pronutro cereal and sugar. All that was required was to add water.

Pronutro was light to carry, but after a few days of not eating anything else it would taste like sweet sawdust.

Of course we would have liked to leave most of the ammo behind as well, but that would be a really crazy thing to do. I remember hearing a story about some guy who used to patrol with only the barrel of a machine gun! He would wear his poncho and the barrel would stick out from under it creating the illusion that the rest of the big gun was hidden.

That however was during the mid-sixties when the war was still a mild affair. In later years only a madman would have risked going on patrol with only a barrel because if the enemy didn't shoot him his own men probably would have. We relied heavily on the firepower of the MAG.

On one of our patrols during the early days of the war, a Chipinga farmer carried so much booze that he sounded like one of the brewery's delivery trucks with all those bottles "clinking" against each other at every step. No one complained about the noise, though. We knew he wouldn't be able to drink all that booze by himself.

Some guys carried little Bibles, some had knives in addition to their bayonets and as the war dragged on, more soldiers started strapping their own pistols around their waists as well. I'm not sure why, but some of the people were quite determined to nail a terrorist with their own handgun instead of their army-issue automatic assault rifle.

I heard a story about an officer I knew, who had purchased an expensive Ruger .44 Magnum revolver and who actually stopped his troops from tossing grenades into a cave where a lone terrorist sought refuge. The officer wanted to plug the enemy with his big handgun.

He did too. Crawled right into that cave knowing full well that the terrorists would be able to see him against the light of the entrance while he would not be able to see the terrorist in the darkness. Of course the terrorist blazed away at him with his AK-47 the minute he entered the cave. That was probably what he expected and wanted to happen because he stayed cool and killed his man with a few well aimed shots in the direction of the muzzle flashes.

I believed that story because I knew the guy. What he had done was typical of him. After all, his party trick was to lie on his back in a slight hollow with a M-962 shrapnel grenade in each hand. He would remove the pins with his teeth and then gently roll the grenades a few paces to either side where they would explode. There was never a scratch on him despite all that shrapnel flying about.

As the war dragged on we learnt the value of having biltong (dried meat), salami, rusks and bread in the bush. Even stale bread isn't that bad when toasted over a fire. The army issue "dog" biscuits weren't bad either despite the fact that the guys used to warn each other to be careful not to drop a biscuit in case it landed on a toe and smashed it.

As we continued on our patrol I kept an eye on the sun which was now starting to descend towards the horizon. That was when I suggested we stop under a huge m*arula* tree for a rest and a cup of coffee. We didn't plan to walk much further that day.

I sat with my back against the tree and studied the map while cousin Ben made the coffee. Then I spotted something very interesting on that map. We were quite close to a farmhouse. I mentioned it to the others and someone suggested we spend the night there.

We all thought that was a brilliant idea except for one thing. We wouldn't be able to get to the farm house before dark, and after dark it would be extremely dangerous. The farmer might shoot us, thinking we were terrorists.

After discussing it, we decided to go there anyway. We then drew matches to see who would have to risk his life by trying to get the farmer to let us in? Mike drew the short match and I was mightily relieved about that.

As we made our way towards the homestead in the moonlight we passed the farm sign and saw that a "Neels Watermeyer" lived there. Half an hour later we were outside the security fence which surrounded the house. Mike handed his weapon to one of us and then took his shirt off. He hoped the farmer would see he was a white man before pulling the trigger. We had many black troops as well, but the enemy had no white troops.

Then Mike took a deep breath and approached the diamond mesh fence while the rest of us hid behind the cover of an anthill and watched anxiously.

I wondered whether he would even get to the fence before some massive and ferocious guard dog charged him and gave the game away. But there was no sign of any hounds and Mike made it all the way to the fence.

Then he started yelling at the top of his voice, "Mister Watermeyer, don't shoot! Rhodesian security forces! Don't shoot!" Mike repeated this continuously while we watched anxiously from our hiding place.

Suddenly all the lights in the house went off!

Then, even worse, we saw a window open and the next minute what looked like a double-barrel shotgun emerged from the opening! Mike to his everlasting credit, didn't budge. He just shouted a bit louder and with more urgency than before.

Then the farmer mercifully shouted, "OK hang on a minute, I'm coming to open the gate for you."

Neels Watermeyer proved to be an outstanding host. He took us into his lounge where, despite his protests, we refused to sit on the beautiful easy chairs because we were so dirty. Instead we parked ourselves on the carpet and he soon took the hint and offered us a bath. We took turns to have a good soak in the tub.

He also slapped a crate of cold "chiboelies" down in front of us so no one spent too much time lying in the bath because we all knew those beers would disappear very quickly. Later he fed us on steak, egg and chips which was a real treat.

We chatted for a long time that night and really enjoyed his company. I think he enjoyed having us there to relieve the loneliness. After being attacked one night he had sent his wife and small children to live with family in Salisbury (now Harare). He told us that for a change he would sleep soundly that night because of our presence.

Neels also told us an incredible story.

Just the week before, he had visited his neighbour and while driving back home again on the gravel road in his open Land Rover late in the afternoon with the wind blowing in his face, he had suddenly heard an almighty explosion behind him! Thinking he was being ambushed he just slammed his foot down on the accelerator in an attempt to drive out of the killing zone as quickly as possible. He heard nothing further and raced home as fast as he could.

When he arrived home, he immediately locked the security gate behind him and ran into the house with his rifle and locked himself in. Then he used the Agric-alert radio to inform the police about what had happened. The policeman he spoke to, told him that as it was already getting dark and because he wasn't in immediate danger, they wouldn't respond to his call until the morning. He also warned Neels to be very careful that night.

At dawn the police arrived with a tracker team. After recounting what had happened the previous day, the Centenary farmer took them in his Land Rover to the place where he had heard the explosion.

Not wanting to spoil any tracks by walking over them, Neels waited in the road by the vehicle with one of the cops while the trackers scouted around. Before long they found the corpse of a terrorist lying on top of the steep bank just above where the Land Rover was parked.

After undressing and examining the body they concluded that he had been killed by a hand-grenade because of all the obvious shrapnel wounds. That puzzled everyone because Neels hadn't tossed a grenade at his attacker. He hadn't retaliated at all.

In fact he hadn't even seen the man.

The trackers did a couple of "three-sixties" (walking in ever wider circles) looking for tracks, but the only ones they found was that of the dead terrorist. They then returned to where the others were waiting by the vehicle.

That was when Neels spotted something which solved the mystery.

He saw a hand-grenade pin lying in the back of his Land Rover. What had apparently happened was that the terrorist had seen him driving past to his neighbour and knowing that he would return by the same route, had decided to ambush him. He had found the perfect ambush site on the bank above the road. All he had to do was drop a grenade into the open Land Rover as it drove past. It was also the perfect time as it would soon be dark and he would have all night to get far away.

After waiting patiently, he had probably seen the dust of Neels's Land Rover approaching. That, in all likelihood, was when he had pulled the grenade's pin out.

Then when Neels's vehicle was directly below him, he had gone into action. But presumably because he was nervous or high on marijuana, he had dropped the pin into the vehicle, and discarded the grenade. Then he had waited for the explosion!

oooOooo

BUSH HAPPY

There was the time we had been on patrol near Marymount Mission on top of the escarpment when "bush happiness" struck us with a vengeance. After weeks of climbing over rugged scorpion and snake-riddled mountains and marching through wasp, mosquito, ant, spider, earwig and thorn infested valleys diligently searching for the enemy, we all suddenly reached our limit.

We wanted to do something different for a change so we held a bush conference to decide what. At that point I remembered the last time we had held a bush conference we decided to play a rugby match in a dry riverbed using a live hand grenade for a ball.

It had been a great game of running rugby with some exceptionally slick handling and passing because no one was prepared to kick the ball. Not only because you might have broken your toe, but also because you might have kicked the pin out of the grenade.

This time thankfully, the lads opted for a party.

On that patrol there were five of us instead of the usual four. There was John Fourie, the cousins Mike Rogers and Greg McIntyre, my cousin Ben and myself. I was in charge but that just meant I was the idiot carrying the heavy radio.

We soon hatched a plan and headed for the nearest kraal where we purchased a scrawny chicken, half a dozen sticks of sugarcane, about a dozen sweet potatoes and a large unhygienic-looking plastic container of "*katjas*."

The latter is an alcoholic brew made mainly from fermented grain of any type, but which can contain anything else as well; like a handful of *marula* fruit, a snake's head, beetle's snout or lizard's tail. Tossing a couple of torch batteries or a wee drop of petrol into *katjas* in an effort to make it more lethal is not unheard of.

By army standards, we had a feast that warm evening under the stars and moon. We washed our food down with huge gulps from the plastic container, which was passed around.

After talking an awful lot of nonsense late into the night we eventually killed the fire, which we weren't supposed to have lit, and went to sleep. I took first guard and as I sat there smoking the cigarette I wasn't supposed to have lit, my mind churned out awfully deep thoughts.

"*Katjas*" tends to make you very wise and philosophical. Especially philosophical. I sat there while everyone else snored around me and wondered who I was and whether or not I really existed?

I always found that whenever I was alone on night guard, my thoughts drifted to my beloved, but that night I caught myself thinking about Mawdy and Horse. They were my first two cows when I had been so poor that I had to tie them to trees in order to milk them.

The very first man on my payroll, Lovemore Station, had named them. I never did find out why he called the one cow Horse. I thought about it a great deal over the years, but I never came up with a satisfactory answer.

Now tanked up with *katjas* I still couldn't explain it, but the realisation did strike me that if anyone was going to call a cow "Horse" it would definitely be someone with a name like Lovemore Station. At that point I realised *katjas* can make you very wise.

I glanced at my luminous watch and saw it was almost time to wake the next guard. The time had flown and I was shocked that I had been sitting on that boulder for so long thinking about my two old bony Jersey cows instead of her! I decided that when we returned to base camp I would have to speak to the cook about the amount of libido-wrecking bluestone he was dumping into our coffee...

I then woke the next guard and crawled into my sleeping bag. I soon drifted off and slept like a dead man until the early hours of the morning when Greg, who was on guard then, woke me up. Of course I immediately grabbed my automatic rifle and started scanning the surroundings for terrorists. After all, for what other reason would the guard wake me up?

But Greg whispered urgently, "No! No! Look up there!"

I looked where he was pointing and couldn't believe what I saw. In fact, what I saw convinced me that I was still fast asleep and in the middle of a fascinating dream.

Up there in the dark sky, with the moon and stars as background, a huge flying saucer hovered.

I pinched myself and was stunned to discover I was wide awake.

The big UFO was quite close and I got the distinct feeling we were being watched. Greg and I woke the other guys up, no doubt because we felt there was safety in numbers. John and Mike soon joined us and were just as flabbergasted, but we couldn't wake cousin Ben.

We tried several times, but each time he became more irate and told us, "Fuck off and leave me alone, I'm tired of your jokes." He was an easy-going guy, but you didn't mess with him when he wanted to sleep. He was rather a big boy and even stronger than he looked.

The four of us huddled together and stared at the strange craft under the full moon not knowing what to make of it. Then John, it could only have been him, suggested we shoot the hell out of it.

"Nooooo," I replied. "What if it shoots back?" Mugabe's terrorists were bad enough, I didn't want a missile or perhaps some strange ray gun having a go at me.

We stared in astonishment at the UFO for about 10 minutes and during that time someone whispered that the strange craft didn't make a sound. I was in such a daze that I hadn't even noticed, but then I listened carefully. I couldn't hear an engine at all. It was eerie, it was surreal. We also noticed that green lights whizzed around and around the centre of the UFO, but we never saw any little green men...

Then suddenly and without warning, the "thing" moved away at an incredible speed until we could no longer see it. I had once called in a Hawker

Hunter air strike and had been impressed with their noise and speed, but the UFO was different...

It was much, much faster and absolutely silent. So much faster than a Hunter jet aircraft that it would be like comparing a cheetah racing with a chameleon.

Despite Ben grumbling, "Go to sleep you noisy bastards," a couple of times, we discussed the saucer for quite a while under the full moon before eventually trying to sleep again.

The next morning we packed up and headed back to base. Our patrol was over and our headaches from the *katjas* were just beginning. Despite our pounding heads, we talked non-stop about the mysterious thing we had seen that night as we walked through the long dew-wet grass.

This eventually became too much for Ben. He was now under the impression that his four comrades had plotted against him.

"Listen, you stupid sods, I know what you are up to and I'm not falling for it so you might as well give up your fucking ridiculous story about a UFO, " he growled.

When we arrived back at camp, we went to the Lieutenant's tent as usual to fill in the patrol report and to be de-briefed. It was my task as sergeant and patrol leader to fill in the report, but everyone was supposed to read and sign it.

One of the questions on the form was "Did you see, hear or notice anything strange during your patrol?"

Normally you would answer that with a simple "No" or "Yes, we saw some Russian boot tracks on a path running alongside the Ruya River heading east. We followed them for two miles but then lost them when it started raining." Or something like that.

But this time I wrote a unique answer, maybe the only such answer in the entire history of Rhodesian Army patrol reports?

I wrote, "Yes, we saw an unidentified flying object hovering near us at 02H30 this morning. The shape of the object was similar to a saucer and it had green lights spinning around it and amazingly it made no sound at all. We watched it for roughly 10 minutes and it then moved off at an incredible speed and without a sound until it disappeared altogether."

When cousin Ben saw what I had written he was horrified. "You can't write that! They'll lock you up in a cell at Brady Barracks (the Rhodesian Army's military prison near Bulawayo) and throw the key away."

At least I had a cousin who cared.

I just smiled at him and gleefully watched his face registering shock as the other three guys read the document and signed it without hesitation. I suspect Ben at that stage thought, "The officer is in on this evil prank," because he soon regained his composure, just shook his head and laughed before saying, "You guys never fucking give up do you?" the Lieutenant arrived and I thought, "Okay Mister Fancy Lieutenant, this is it. You can think I've lost my marbles, but I have three witnesses which should make this clash very interesting."

He read my report, looked up and calmly said, "Did you guys see it as well?"

The bewildered look on Ben's face at that moment will remain in my mind and amuse me forever.

The platoon commander informed us that the camp guard had woken everyone in the base up during the early hours of the morning and that they had all gone outside to look at the UFO. He went on to explain that the flying saucer hadn't been near them, it had been in the distance. That made perfect sense to us because we had been "in the distance" too.

"What do you think it was, Sir?" I enquired politely.

"I don't have a clue," he replied."

oooOooo

SAVED BY RUBBISH

After only one night at Rusambo our platoon was sent to set up a base in the area and patrol from there. We drove the Bedford trucks and Land Rover into really dense bush and our officer then allocated us our all-round defensive positions. At that time each platoon had a Land Rover, but later when land mines became more numerous these vehicles were left behind for use on tarred roads only.

I will never forget that first night at our new base camp. We were sleeping in a defensive circle and I found myself under a nice shady fuchsia tree which made me both happy and worried.

Fushsia trees, also known as weeping boerboon or *mutondochuru* (by the Shona people), produce nectar in such quantity that it even drips from the tree and I was under it! Also the sweet nectar attracts birds which of course attract snakes.

Still, it was nice to be in the shade as that part of the world can be extremely hot.

At about two in the morning that first night, I was jolted from my sleep by someone screaming. It was no ordinary scream. It was the scream of a traumatised person. One of those very rare blood-curdling screams that the majority of people never hear.

I immediately thought we were being attacked by terrorists and grabbed my FN and cocked it. I heard other rifles being cocked all around the camp. During those first years of the war we only cocked our rifles when necessary. Later on we carried cocked rifles all the time with the safety catch on.

The fearful screaming continued and at that point I thought, "There's no shooting. They must have infiltrated the camp and are cutting someone's throat with a blunt knife?"

Later we found out what had happened.

Dennis van Zyl had woken up and decided he would have a cigarette. We weren't allowed to smoke after dark, but everyone did. Dennis knew he had left his smokes and lighter next to him and still half-asleep, had lazily stretched out an arm to grab the packet.

Instead he curled his fingers around a snake!

Judging by what he felt in his hand he knew this was a big brute of a snake too. Not that size matters much. Little snakes can be just as deadly as big snakes.

While Dennis's mind was still grappling with the shock of realising what he held firmly in his hand, the snake, no doubt objecting to being harassed by a total stranger, wrapped itself around his arm a few times.

That was when Dennis went berserk. He leapt up and started screaming blue murder. At the same time he dashed around in the dark furiously shaking and swinging his arm in a desperate effort to get rid of the venomous serpent.

John Sly, who was the closest to Dennis, woke up confused and like everyone else grabbed and cocked his rifle. Attracted by the noise he then spotted Dennis who was galloping around the camp like a crazed stallion with turpentine under its tail, and aimed at him. John continued to follow the man with his weapon wondering whether he was friend or foe?

Then poor old Dennis started running straight at John!

John later swore he had already started squeezing the trigger when Dennis fell into the rubbish pit.

The fall probably saved Dennis's life in two ways. He didn't get shot by his comrade, and the big snake came off his arm and disappeared into the night.

A few minutes later, order was restored in the camp and the officer started questioning Dennis. After listening to his story, the Lieutenant, like most of us, was sceptical.

"Bullshit man! Nothing happened. You had a fucking nightmare," he growled.

Officers, despite having undisturbed sleep unlike the rest of who had to do guard duties, became a bit irate when suddenly jolted from peaceful slumber by insane screaming in the early hours of the morning.

Not to mention the scare of him thinking the Battle of Armageddon had begun like the rest of us.

Dennis was quite indignant to be accused of "only having had a nightmare" and he had a go at the officer, something which was not recommended because officers, whom we often called "ossifers" behind their backs, could and would lay a charge against you if they suspected you were being insubordinate. That could result in a spell in the military prison at Brady Barracks or, at best having to dig a latrine pit while your buddies lay around loafing.

"Oh yes? Explain to me what bit me on the forehead then, Sir." Dennis spat the "Sir" out in a tone, which fringed on dangerous disrespect.

"You were bitten by the snake?" the Lieutenant asked sarcastically.

"Sarge fetch my torch pronto, it's lying on my trunk in the tent," he ordered. Our commander's tone of voice clearly indicated he was confident that he was about to expose Dennis as a liar.

When the torch arrived the Lieutenant grabbed it impatiently, switched it on and shone it into Dennis's face.

In the middle of his forehead we saw two distinct drops of blood. They were more or less the same width apart as would be a big snake's fangs.

Our medic examined the puncture marks and then told the officer that he didn't think the snake could have injected much venom into his victim.

"The bone is so close to the skin there, Sir, that the snake's head must have bounced off," he announced.

I always suspected old Dennis was a bit of a bonehead.

Dennis said he felt OK, but firmly told his now very sympathetic officer that under no circumstances was he going back to sleep in his all-round defensive position. The officer let the shaken man spend the rest of the night sleeping inside the Land Rover's cab and ordered the medic to check up on his condition at regular intervals.

The rest of us, however, had to return to our all round defensive positions. I settled down under my tree, but I struggled to go back to sleep because I knew that snake was still around. Each time I started drifting off to sleep something would fall out of the tree and I would jerk awake and that's how a macho part-time soldier turned into a wimp, at least until dawn.

oooOooo

THE SILENT ENEMY

There were two things I hated with a passion in the army: Guard duty and night ambushes. The enemy came a poor third. Guard duty during my national service spell years earlier at Llewellyn Barracks wasn't too bad. There were always two of us guarding the ammunition dump. Although we weren't allowed to, one guy would stroll around inside the perimeter fence for an hour while the other slept on top of the hand grenade cases inside the tent. Then we swapped roles.

The late Alan Vaughan and myself would talk about serious things whenever we were on guard together, which was often. I recall the time we made the pact.

During the early hours of the morning we started talking about the possibility of being wounded or killed and at first neither of us was overly concerned.

I said, "I don't think you even know it if you get shot in the head."

"No, it will be like being knocked out forever."

Then we made the mistake of discussing being shot in the genitals.

Now that was a horrifying thought for both of us and before our two-hour guard spell was over we had made the pact. We each solemnly pledged to shoot the other stone dead if either of us was ever shot "down there." That eased my mind considerably. I now had an "insurance policy" which guaranteed a steel-point bullet in my brain if ever I was so unlucky. Alan was a good buddy and I knew he would keep his promise, as much as I intended to keep mine.

Ambushes were even worse than guard duties.

Not only were you expected to stay awake all night, you also had to be very quiet, which meant no talking, coughing or going to the toilet. Of course you were allowed to pee in your pants where you lay as long - as you did it very quietly and didn't sigh with relief afterwards.

I learnt that there was no substitute for experience when it came to ambushing. Over the years I learnt a few helpful tricks. Firstly, the thing was to use a hand and sweep the area where you were about to lie down. If you didn't do that you would discover you were lying on a tiny pebble under your poncho which would "grow and grow" all night until it felt like a massive granite boulder under you. And tiny dry twigs could turn into gigantic logs after a few hours.

The trick was to get rid of anything before you lay down and while everyone else was still getting into position as well. During that short spell there would be the sound of twigs snapping or being crunched, some rustling noise and the rattle of the machine gun belt being unrolled and no one would notice you sweeping away.

If you did it later after everyone was settled, the person in charge would hear you fidgeting and get extremely annoyed.

While clearing away pebbles and twigs you had to do a little praying for "no scorpions please" as your hand swept the ground in the dark. If a scorpion nailed you the ambush would be as good as over because you would no doubt scream like a stuck pig from the intense pain.

Maybe the leader would have understood why you screamed and compromised the ambush. But perhaps not, for officers were funny in that way.

It wouldn't matter to an officer if he himself snored so loudly that an elephant cow in the distance thought it was a mating call and answered with a loud trumpet. However, if he was awake and you fidgeted just a little bit by scratching your ear where a mosquito had bitten it, he would threaten to put you on a charge.

Officers were like that.

One dark night in the Mukumbura area we headed towards our ambush site with a Bedford truck. Due to sound carrying such a long way at night, the truck didn't stop when we reached our drop zone. We reasoned that the local villagers would hear the truck stopping and report our presence to the terrorists so our driver merely slowed down and we jumped off the back. Giovanni Bergamasco stumbled when his feet hit the road and he ended up with his nose in the gravel. The rest of us laughed so loudly that it might have been better if the truck had stopped.

We waited for Giovanni to dust himself down, wipe the blood from his nose and clean the barrel of his machine gun and then we set off through the bush towards the ambush site some five miles away. We had been ordered to ambush a store which Army Intelligence had assured us would be robbed and burnt to the ground that very night. We weren't very concerned such a thing would actually happen because experience had taught us that Army Intelligence was seldom correct. But there were rare exceptions to that rule.

As we walked as quietly as possible through the bush, I wondered why they were called Army Intelligence? Something like Military Fantasies Unit would have been far more accurate.

My thoughts about Army Intelligence reminded me of the man we called Charlie Grid Square. He was a spotter plane pilot who thought he had the eyesight of an eagle. Charlie would fly around in circles and see the most incredible things. Then he would radio us on the ground and send us miles away to check out what he had spotted.

A terrorist he had seen leaning against a rock on top of a high mountain would turn out to be the shadow of a dead tree that had fallen over. The movement he had seen in a forest would be two impala rams locking horns and so on.

After responding to many such wild goose chases we started saluting Charlie whenever he flew past. The salute would consist of a row of guys bent over with their shorts around their ankles...

Charlie Grid Square probably thought he had seen a group of albino hippos which each only had one eye.

When we eventually reached the store my thoughts returned to the present and soon I knew our ambush was in trouble. There was no cover around the store except for a row of scraggly little msasa bushes directly in front of the building's entrance.

At least the lack of cover made it easy to decide where we were going to set the ambush.

We sneaked into the msasas in single file and found positions. I remembered to do my "quick sweep" trick with my hand.

After settling down, I peered at the store's whitewashed walls over my rifle barrel and decided that we weren't in such a bad position after all – just a bit too close to the target. But I found I was quite comfortable.

Then the smell hit me.

It was awful and I was worried because I wasn't sure where it was coming from.

That was when good old Bob Jones, lying a meter away on my right, provided the answer by groaning, "I'm lying right on a fresh turd and it's squashed all over my chest!"

Bob was my hero. He was such a great guy to have around. Without fail, he always took the punishment whenever any was handed out. To me Bob was like a bullet-proof vest. If ever one of us was going to be shot in the bush, I just knew it would be him.

The few words he had uttered sounded so sweet to me. The smell was terrible, but at least I knew I wasn't the one lying on the source of it.

I found I was in deep water because I realised I was going to laugh and wouldn't be able to stop myself. Bob started muttering and I started giggling and between the two of us we made quite a din.

The Lieutenant on my left became extremely annoyed. He was known for having a short fuse and just then he was on the verge of exploding.

"For fuck's sake, shut up you two morons," he whispered in a menacing tone.

I did, but not for long before I was overcome with another fit of laughter. Bob muttered some more as well.

That was when the officer almost lost it. "What the hell are you two doing?" He sounded extremely irritated and the vision of a prison cell door shutting flashed through my mind.

In a low whisper I explained Bob's problem to him. There was a short spell of silence and then he also started giggling. Hearing their officer laughing encouraged the other guys to enquire about what was happening and after he told them, they also eventually started laughing uncontrollably.

After a while we settled down to clandestine mode again. It proved to be a terrible night because the smell was always around, but the fact that Bob and not yours truly was lying on it helped a great deal. For whatever reason, the enemy never came and about an hour before dawn we abandoned our ambush and walked back to the road where the truck driver had arranged to meet us.

We made Bob sit at the tail end of the truck while we huddled behind the cab. We laughed and laughed all the way back to camp and Bob cursed and cursed.

In camp, Bob immediately removed his shirt and washed himself. He then joined us around the fire and someone handed him a glass of neat brandy to cheer him up. He downed it and was instantly back to his usual jocular self. He was that kind of guy.

oooOooo

WATERFALL

Most Rhodesians who lived in the Manicaland province could speak a little Shona, but it was a rare few who could speak the language as well as, if not better than, the Shonas themselves.

Piet Bornman was one of those and on rare occasions we used him to eavesdrop on the locals' gossip at night in the hope of him hearing something that would help us to find the terrorists.

One dark night, we sent Piet in to eavesdrop on a couple living in a newly-built lone hut in the Hippo Valley area while we covered him from a bit further away.

Eavesdropping like that could be near impossible when there were dogs around. The half-starved mutts would bark non-stop at the intruder until someone with a spear would come and investigate.

During a day patrol a week before, we had visited the couple and had noticed there were no dogs around. We had also noticed their surly and uncooperative manner towards us and thought that might be because they were sympathetic to, and collaborating with, the terror gang operating in that area.

When the man and woman moved away from the embers of the fire and entered their hut we sent Piet with his camouflage cream streaked face closer.

He sneaked in next to the hut and lay there among the bushes listening. He later told us they never spoke about anything controversial, but that he would remember the night for a long time.

He lay there for half an hour listening to them chatting loudly and then suddenly he heard the hut door being opened. He saw the woman come out and he hugged the ground a bit closer so that she wouldn't see him. He kept his eyes on her though and then saw her turn left from the entrance and start walking in his direction...

When he realised she was striding directly towards him he went cold...

She walked right up to him and just as Piet thought she was going to step on him, she stopped and turned around. He could see her ankles right in front of his eyes and the hem of her dress was almost touching the top of his head. He tried to pull his head back into his shoulders like a tortoise and held his breath.

The woman then hitched up her skirt and squatted down. She was so close to him that her bum was almost touching his face. Piet lay there, frozen.

Then she started peeing.

At that moment Piet said he closed his eyes. Not because he was a gentleman, but because he could feel tiny drops of urine splashing onto his face and didn't want it in his eyes as well.

She must have been holding it for a long time because the waterfall went on and on for what seemed an eternity. The woman eventually stopped and just squatted there for a while drip-drying. Finally she stood up, dropped her dress down and walked back to the hut totally unaware that she had almost drowned a Rhodesian soldier.

oooOooo

SECRET WEAPON

We were driving through really thick bush when a tree branch caught on the cab of the Bedford and bent back. Fortunately our driver stopped and warned us to be careful when that branch came loose because it was going to whip across the back of the truck where we were sitting and behead anyone sitting upright.

We all ducked down really low and the driver moved the truck forward. "Whoosh" the thick branch flashed just above our heads and I clearly heard it strike something. I looked up and couldn't believe what I saw!

My cousin Jaco's FN rifle barrel was bent almost 90 degrees obviously from the impact of the branch. He had ducked down, but had unfortunately left his FN rifle wedged in an upright position between the steel seat and the tailgate.

Jaco had to endure an awful lot of joking about his damaged rifle. I recall someone telling him he would now be able to shoot around corners. Another guy said, "Jaco if there's a terrorist on the other side of a boulder you can just hold your rifle against the side of the rock and shoot him."

When the Major saw his rifle he just shook his head and said, "It would be yours wouldn't it?" He had that kind of a reputation.

ooooOoooo

BLOW UP PRACTICE

To this day I don't believe it is necessary to practice being blown up, but that is precisely what we did once during the few days training before we went to the border. We had to drive along a dirt road and then every now and again, when we least expected it, an instructor would blow us up with plastic explosives placed in holes in the road. He would also fire blanks at us immediately after the explosion.

The idea was for us to practice getting off the truck quickly after being blown up by landmine and then attacking the ambushing enemy in pairs. One man shooting while the other moves.

Although the loud bang gave us all a fright the first time wasn't too bad. However it seemed the instructor really enjoyed seeing us jump when the explosion went off just in front of the truck so he insisted on doing it again and again. That wouldn't have been too bad, but he kept on using more and more plastic explosive...

Tempers were getting frayed because each time we were "blown up" rocks and sand rained down on us.

We started complaining bitterly so the instructor said, "Okay just one more time."

He must have put all his remaining plastic explosive into the last hole because when he detonated it he blew the windscreen right out of the Bedford truck! Fortunately no one was injured.

We had the last laugh because he had to pay for the repairs.

ooooOoooo

PINNED

By modern standards, ours wasn't a high-tech war by any stretch of the imagination. We used mainly rifles and machine-guns. Our aircraft were "yesteryear" planes too. We even patched up and used Vampire jets that had previously been in a museum.

As the war dragged on and more and more men were drafted into the army, Second World War Bren guns were re-introduced and issued to them and you occasionally saw men in uniform with ancient Lee-Enfield bolt-action .303 rifles. The police issued me with a Sten gun to enable me to protect myself on the farm and at first I was impressed because it had a 32-round magazine. However, after trying it out I soon realised it was a piece of junk compared to my own arsenal of hunting weapons and especially my army-issue FN rifle.

I recall once standing chatting to the Sergeant Major on the banks of the Sabi River near Chisumbanje when suddenly a Bren gun nearby fired a burst over the water.

Nothing unusual about that except no one was near the gun at the time.

It was just lying there with the butt on the ground and the barrel suspended in the air by the bipod underneath. We made the weapon safe and then examined it. We discovered that the tiny piece of metal which was supposed to hold the breech block and firing pin mechanism back had been worn so badly the working parts slipped over it from time to time.

Everyone was grateful it hadn't been pointing in their direction.

We also carried and used Second World War Mills grenades at first, but later these were replaced by American M-962 shrapnel grenades. In addition we each carried a white phosphorous grenade. We also carried rifle grenades, first the Energa grenade and then later what we knew as the 32-Zulu.

Firing a rifle grenade was easy if you knew what you were doing. You took the magazine off and made sure you removed the bullet in the chamber. Then you loaded a special balistite cartridge and rammed the grenade over the end of the barrel.

You also had to be aware that firing a rifle grenade delivered a hefty kick which was worse than firing a .458 calibre rifle designed for shooting jumbo, rhino and buffalo. The trick was to remember not to put the butt into your shoulder, but under your arm against your hip or on the ground in a "mortar" firing position.

Most important – it was vital not to stick your trigger finger into the trigger guard and around the trigger as you normally would. Instead you held your hand on the side of the trigger guard and then merely tickled the side of the trigger with your thumb, making sure you didn't insert it right over the trigger.

I had fired several rifle grenades during my national service and knew exactly what to do, but when I first joined 4th Infantry Battalion I found no one there had ever fired one. Then I watched a rather pompous officer attempt to fire a rifle grenade for the first time.

He held the rifle in the correct position, but then I saw him slip his thumb deeply into the trigger guard. I thought of warning him, but then I remembered he was an officer.

Bang! The grenade flew off the end of the barrel and landed right on the old car wreck we were using for a target and exploded in a plume of black smoke.

Then I looked at the officer and could see he was in agony. He was holding his hand in front of his eyes and his thumb was bent right back – dislocated.

Besides rifle grenades, most of us had been trained to fire bazookas but after my national service I never saw one again. I suppose they would have been issued to us had the enemy tried to cross the border with tanks. Towards the end of the war when the possible use of enemy tanks did become a mild threat, several 25 pounder artillery guns were apparently positioned in the Vumba mountains overlooking the road from Beira in Mozambique.

I am sure our Eland armoured cars with their 90 mm guns and the Unimogs with their mounted 106 mm recoilless rifles had the ability to deal with tanks as well. Towards the end of the war, we had acquired about twenty of our own Russian T-55 tanks. These were apparently captured in Mozambique.

One weapon we carried and which proved to be highly effective in an ambush was the claymore mine. I loved them because they had the potential to reduce enemy numbers significantly and they made such a loud bang that the enemy was bound to be confused for a few seconds. And seconds inside an ambush killing zone were an eternity.

With claymore mines you just had to be careful where you positioned yourself because they had a vicious back blast.

Then there was the Pookie, which was hardly high-tech. It was a little vehicle designed and built to locate landmines. It had a metal detector wing on each side and I was told its extremely wide tyres were filled with helium. It meant a Pookie could drive over a mine without setting it off and at the same time the metal detectors would locate the mine, unless it was a Chinese wood and glue mine.

Whenever the Pookie's sensors detected a mine, the driver would stop immediately and switch on the flashing rear lights to warn the vehicles behind him. The driver would then dig in the road with his bayonet in an effort to find the mine. More often than not, he found an old Coke can.

Compared to more developed nations, we used extremely outdated weapons. My generation of troops and those before us, did their national service with old 7,62 mm British SLRs. After a few months at Llewellyn Barracks we had to hand the SLRs in and were given brand new 7,62 mm FNs (Fabrique Nationale) still covered in grease.

We had to bathe those rifles in hot water to remove the grease and then we smeared a tiny bit of abrasive grease on the breech block so that it would become a bit looser after shooting with them.

We were so proud of those rifles and we liked the fact that they were slightly shorter than our previous weapons. The "bonus" about them was the bayonet proved to be an outstanding bottle opener.

We had to ditch the slings, though, because the army didn't want us patrolling with our weapons slung, they wanted us to walk with our rifles in a ready-to-fire position. Our army was never one which cared much for the comfort of infantry soldiers.

In the Rhodesian Army your rifle was always a rifle and never a gun. If you made the mistake of calling it a gun, you had to chant, "This is my rifle (grabbing your rifle) and this is my gun (grabbing your crotch), this is for shooting (grabbing your rifle) and this (grabbing your crotch) is for fun".

Much later and wise by hindsight, I realise that you have to be philosophical about most things. The FN and SLR were the same calibre and both had a 20-round magazine. The real difference was that the FN could be set on fully-automatic while the SLR was a semi-automatic.

It is arguable whether fully-automatic is an advantage. On automatic the FN was not very accurate and you could run out of ammunition in no time.

No matter what weapon one uses the bottom line is "Death is death". It simply doesn't matter what kills.

No one ever asks, "Did you kill me with a musket or a cruise missile?"

I fully realised that the day we saw the dead terrorist in Luke Wentworth's compound with the arrow still sticking out of his back. The guineafowl feathers at the end of the arrow fluttered in the breeze.

A farm labourer shot the gook with his bow and arrow one night. The terrorists had arrived in the farm compound and demanded food and beer. After a few hours of heavy drinking they didn't even notice one of their hosts had sneaked off to fetch his weapon. If anyone had seen him leave, he would have told them he was just going for a leak.

From the shelter of the dark shadows he drew the bowstring back as far as he could and took careful aim. He watched his arrow fly straight and true and strike deeply into his target, before beating a hasty retreat into the dark bush.

He had no family and therefore didn't even bother to risk going back after the other terrorists had fled. He spent an uncomfortable night in the bush and the next morning he made his way towards the police station on the hill in Odzi to claim his reward.

He had decided to become a bounty hunter after reading the Government pamphlets stuck on the walls of the post office and which offered cash rewards for terrorists – dead or alive. There were also cash rewards offered for handing in an AK-47 or any other terrorist weapon.

The bounty hunter was a simple illiterate farm worker who with a single twang of his bowstring had earned the equivalent of more than 40 years salary.

He might have been an ordinary brave worker, but he wasn't stupid. He knew the terrorists would kill him as soon as they could, so the first thing he did with his money was buy a train ticket to Salisbury where no one knew him.

A rich man can easily lose himself in a big city.

oooOooo

WEIGHT IS ONLY A NUMBER

When I think back now, the most exciting times during the war were being on the Zambezi River, going on external operations into a neighbouring country and when I was a member of what we knew as the "Fire Force." This outfit was a group of attack helicopters. Ours, which was based at Mtoko, operated in the Operation Hurricane area and consisted of six French Alouette choppers. Five of them were armed with Browning .303 machine-guns and one, called a K-car, with a massive 20 mm cannon. Due to the weight of the cannon, the K-car only carried the pilot, the gunner and the Fire Force commander. The other choppers each had a pilot, gunner and four troops.

Being part of the Fire Force was really nice for us infantrymen who were used to spending most of our time in the bush walking tremendous distances. We usually walked 63 miles in a three-day patrol and that often included going over high mountains. As members of the Fire Force, we were in base most of the time, either playing darts in the tent, volleyball outside or just sitting around chatting. In the evenings we would drink plenty of beer in the canteen.

Each morning after breakfast we had a muster parade, but no one was interested in whether you had shaved properly or whether your boots were clean. They were only interested in whether your rifle was clean and oiled.

We weren't allowed to leave the camp, but apart from that we could pretty much do as we pleased with one exception - we always had to be ready to board the choppers very quickly.

If the siren sounded we just grabbed our rifles and gear and ran for where the aircraft were waiting. It usually took us only about a minute or two before we were in the air.

The pouches of our combat waistcoats contained six loaded magazines (with a seventh one on the rifle). We also carried a bandolier of a further 50 rounds while a shrapnel grenade and a white phosphorous grenade hung from the webbing at the top in front of the vest. At the back, at the bottom hung two full water bottles. Inside the bottom back pouch, you either had a claymore mine or a 32-Z rifle grenade tucked away together with your cigarettes.

Above that pouch your sleeping bag was strapped on usually with a quarter bottle of whisky or brandy nestling safely inside it. The top back pouch contained three days' rations.

Between the four of us in our group we would also have a smoke grenade, a light grenade, two gas stoves, some spare gas cylinders, spare radio batteries and a tiny medical pack. Each troopie always carried a wound dressing. The section leader had the radio and some mini-flares.

The guy with the 7.62 mm machine-gun was never asked to carry anything else because he was already carrying the most weight.

The Fire Force system proved to be highly effective, especially when it was first introduced. What happened was that four-man OPs (observation points) would be established on mountains and kopjes and the men would take turns scanning the area below them with powerful binoculars for any sign of the enemy. At the same time patrols would take place in an attempt to get the terrorists to move around so they could be spotted.

If the OPs spotted anything or a patrol ran into any kind of trouble they couldn't handle themselves, they would radio the base and ask for the Fire Force. In a chopper you could get to the action so much quicker. You could also see so much more from the sky.

The drill was for the aircraft to locate and engage the enemy and also drop troops off in stop-group positions. In theory, the aircraft would attack and kill the terrorists and any who managed to escape would hopefully run into the ambushes nearby.

The Fire Force commander could also, by radio, order troops to move when it appeared that the enemy were on the run in a direction where there wasn't a stop-group. In addition, he could order troops to move in closer and engage the enemy from the ground as well if and when they made a stand.

That didn't happen often because the airmen, who we called "Blue Jobs," were real professionals. They usually did all the hard stuff themselves and us "Brown Jobs" were grateful for that. I always admired the cool and collected way in which the airmen went about their work. To me they were quite amazing.

During the heat of battle they would chat away on their radios in such a casual manner that one would have thought they were sitting on a beach with a beer discussing a pretty girl in a bikini who had walked past. Not much seemed to ruffle them.

I found I could never do that. When the bullets started flying all I could think of was self-preservation. Shoot the bastard before he shoots you. The first few seconds were always the worst and then the adrenaline kicked in and calmed me down.

That didn't mean I was no longer thinking of self-preservation, it just meant I was calmly thinking of self-preservation.

Andy Robertson, a Rhodesian chopper pilot I flew with was once shot in the thigh when he tried to drop troops too close to the enemy. Even then he kept his cool!

He flew that whirly-bird out of the danger zone before landing it and being flown to hospital by another chopper.

After he had recovered he flew again, but first insisted on having a steel plate welded onto the outside of his pilot's seat. The steel would stop an AK-47 bullet from slicing into his thigh again, but it was actually ridiculous because there was nothing to stop a round from hitting the rest of him including his head.

We mocked him about that, but he just said, "They can shoot me in the chest or head, but they are never going to shoot me in the thigh again. Do you know how sore it is to be shot in the thigh?"

If any terrorists escaped from a contact it was our duty to track them and keep reporting back to the Fire Force commander on our progress or lack of it. Depending on circumstances, he would consider sending a chopper with fresh trackers to replace the guys who were tired or dropping more stop-group troops ahead of the terrorists.

The helicopters proved to be highly effective killing machines. The first time I looked through the sights of a mounted twin Browning .303 machine-gun, I couldn't see anything, but the gunner taught me to look "through" the sights and focus beyond them and when I did that the target suddenly became crystal clear. I was also able to clearly see the cross-hairs of the sight. Those gunners all seemed to have the ability to shoot at and hit a man-sized target from the sky without any problem at all.

From time to time a chopper was shot down or ended up with a couple of holes in the fuselage. But that didn't happen often. During the war those little gunships killed many, many terrorists and proved to be ideal for the particular type of war in which we were involved.

Towards the end of the war we acquired some bigger second-hand Bell helicopters from the Israelis, as well, but sadly I never flew in them. I imagine their value lay in the fact that they could transport far more troops than the Alouettes.

Sometimes the Fire Force was called out after the terrorists had murdered a tribesman or woman somewhere. The murders usually took place at night and then we would be dropped off at the scene of the crime at dawn. Whoever was doing the tracking would circle the area until he found tracks and then we would follow the gang while the choppers waited on the ground.

I recall Neville Barlow tracking a gang all day and then he suddenly stopped and beckoned us to come closer. When we reached him, he whispered to us to be extremely alert because we were only minutes behind the enemy. Having done my fair share of hunting and tracking I was sceptical of his warning because I hadn't seen any tracks for quite a while. I suspected he had lost the tracks and didn't want to admit it so I asked him how he knew we were so close behind the gooks?

He didn't answer. Instead he bent down and picked up a tiny piece of sugarcane and handed it to me. Despite the blazing sun that chewed piece of cane was still wet with saliva. I never doubted his tracking ability again.

We were very alert after that despite our weariness. We knew that if the killers were aware we were on their trail, the chances were high that we would be ambushed soon. Not long after finding the sugarcane, we crossed over the border into Mozambique without permission.

Then it was time for me to radio a sitrep (situation report) back and I was excited because I was sure we would be fighting within the next half an hour or so. I updated the commander and he told me to "Wait one, Roger over."

Next minute, his boss, the Operation Hurricane commander, who was known as "Zero," came on the air and ordered us to, "Get out of there immediately!"

The order took us by surprise and I thought perhaps he didn't understand how close we were behind the terror gang so I tried to persuade him to change his mind. That was a huge mistake and when he spoke again I could clearly hear he was very annoyed I had dared to question his order. He sternly repeated his order adding "that is a direct order soldier."

It was laughable. We believed that he thought our presence inside Mozambique might cause an international incident. What other reason could there have been for his order?

We trudged back across the border cursing him because we thought it was crazy that we could have caused an international incident out there in an extremely remote corner of Mozambique. We were right in the middle of nowhere.

Maybe we were naive, but we figured we could have engaged the enemy and then brought the choppers overhead so easily and wiped them out. We later discovered that because of global pressures and ongoing negotiations the politicians had placed a ban, albeit a temporary one, on cross-border attacks. So those terrorists lived to kill again. What a bummer.

After a while a chopper arrived to fetch us and we clambered aboard and flew to an army base camp where we refuelled from a drum. Fuel drums were often left in bases for the helicopters, but once the seal on a drum was broken the choppers wouldn't use a single drop from that drum again. I guess they just didn't want to take any chances that the fuel might be contaminated.

The sun was setting and our South African pilot, Piet Nel, told us with a stern face that he had never flown at night before and would be flying very high to avoid crashing into the mountains in the dark.

He added that if I or any of my men started feeling weird and was about to faint from lack of oxygen, I was to tap him on the shoulder!

I had become used to the pilot's pranks by then and burst out laughing. We really liked that guy despite him being a "Blue Job" and "Slope" to boot. We called the South Africans "Slopes" and they called us "Hairy Backs."

The name "Slope" was derived from someone saying that whenever anything puzzled a South African, which was often, he would slam a palm onto his sloping forehead and say, "Fuck, what now?"

What we liked most about Piet Nel was he never spoke down to anyone despite the fact that he was an officer (Flight Lieutenant). Whenever we landed back at our base camp after a hard day of tramping through the bush, he always led us straight to the canteen and bought us each an ice-cold beer.

No wonder we liked him.

There were two Fire Forces operating in the Operation Hurricane area and early one morning we were ordered to move to a more central point for the day because the other Fire Force helicopters were being serviced. We studied the map and realised where we were going to spend the day there was absolutely nothing but a little dam surrounded by bush.

That was when Piet Nel suggested to me that we load plenty of beer into the chopper. The lads didn't need a second invitation and soon our chopper was crammed with crates of Lion Lager.

One-by-one the choppers took to the air and then it was our turn. The revs and noise level went sky-high as we attempted lift-off, but it was all in vain. The chopper stayed put on the tar.

"Too much weight," I heard Piet say into my headphone.

"OK, switch off and we'll unload some of the beer," I replied.

"No ways," he said, "Don't worry, I have a plan."

It was a good one too. He ran the Alouette down the runway at speed like a fixed wing aircraft and then slowly, but surely we lifted into the air and followed the other choppers, which were already quite a distance from us.

We flew just above the trees, well below the other five aircraft, and to this day I'm not sure whether it was because of the weight or because the likeable slope pilot was trying to fool us as usual?

We didn't take any more chances though, when we returned that evening the chopper was light as a feather.

oooOooo

THE JINXED DECOY MAN

Bob Jones was an unlucky man. Whenever anything bad happened to anyone in our platoon you could be sure he would be involved. The first time I noticed he was jinxed was when some troopers were unloading a huge chest deep-freeze from the back of a truck. It slipped and zonked Bob in the eye. He sported that black eye for a long while.

Then there was the time when we were camped around an old building which, before the war, had been used by the District Commissioner as a rest camp. There were only 17 guys in the platoon that particular time and because of the odd number, Bob found himself alone under a tree in the defensive circle. He was nervous and no one blamed him because there was an awful lot of terrorist activity in the area.

After the first night, Bob told us he hadn't closed an eye and was going to ensure that he slept well in future. He spent the entire day rigging a home-made alarm. He strung some fishing line at about knee-height some 20 yards in front of his position then gave it a 90-degree turn around a twig and through a pulley before eventually leading it to the tree above him. From there it went through another small pulley and then ended up going downwards through a hole in a tin. The line was tied to a rock which hung just below the tin.

When he had completed his contraption he called us to come and inspect it. That was probably a mistake.

We tested it and although I didn't say so, I was impressed. If anyone approached Bob's position from the bush and walked into that line, the rock slammed up into the tin with a loud "clunk." I knew that thin fishing line would be invisible in the dark for sure.

However, someone mentioned something about "the gooks are probably watching you right now and tonight they will come and cut the line and the rock will drop quietly to the ground. Then, Bob, they will cut your throat with a blunt knife while you sleep."

It was only a joke, but Bob, who was probably a bit grumpy from lack of sleep, didn't laugh. Instead he went back to work, modifying his alarm. He was only satisfied after he had rigged a second tin below the rock.

That night as everyone except the guard on duty slept, a loud "clunk" from the direction where Bob was bedded down woke us all. I grabbed my weapon and slipped the safety catch off. I could hear movement around me as other troopers did the same. Then the guy on guard checked to find out what had happened.

He spotted a dog scavenging around and immediately knew the mutt had set off Bob's alarm. He also noticed something else that was very interesting....

Bob's alarm had woken everyone in the camp – except Bob! He was still fast asleep and snoring gently. He had to take a lot of flak from the guys about that the next morning.

During another spell in the bush some months later, we were in our base camp one morning when a young Shona picannin (boy) walked into our camp with a dirt-smeared letter in his hand. It was addressed to "The Rhodesian Security Forces" and was from a terrorist gang leader who was arrogant enough to sign the letter although it obviously wasn't his real name.

The pseudo names the terrorists sometimes used amused me. Names like Bloodsucker, Terror, Black Napoleon, or Axe Killer. Once when I was bored,

I thought if I were a terrorist my name would have been Ball Gnasher. Now that would have frightened the daylights out of the Rhodesian troops.

In the letter, the gang leader gook challenged us to a fight down at the Ruya River at four o'clock that same afternoon!

We laughed ourselves stupid. What was the world and the war coming to? We spend years away from our loved ones roaming the bush looking for those evil bastards who spend years hiding from us. Now suddenly they challenge us to a battle at a specific place and at a specific time.

We all knew they wouldn't be there and so did the Lieutenant, but he said we still had to check it out just in case. What we couldn't figure out was why they wanted us there at that time? They were obviously planning to something really nasty somewhere else...

The officer sent patrols out in all directions that day and Bob and I and two other guys ended up being sent down to the Ruya for the gunfight.

As we walked through the bush towards the river, I started thinking about Bob's bad luck and thought that maybe this wasn't a hoax. Maybe the enemy would be waiting for us? There would probably be 600 of them and the terrorist leader would be spitting mad and would feel insulted that we had only sent four troopers.

144

Rhodesian rivers can be very misleading. The Ruya, for instance, was one of many rivers that became a raging torrent during the rainy season and then a dry sandy stretch during the long, dry winter. It was winter at the time and the Ruya had hardly any water in it, just small green slimy pools full of Bilharzhias snails here and there between the reeds and rocks.

Instead of patrolling on one or both banks of the river where the bush was almost impenetrable, we strolled down the dry river bed. By then I was absolutely convinced we weren't going to find anyone, but Bob must have thought differently? Maybe he didn't and was just a far more conscientious and better soldier than me. I did notice that the other two guys were just as relaxed as I was.

After we had walked a couple of miles with Bob checking behind every bush and rock and slowing us down, he found a crevice in a rock high up on the eastern bank. He asked me to wait while he checked it out.

"Aaah, c'mon Bob," I said impatiently, "there's nothing in there. Let's go man."

"No," he replied, "there might be an arms cache hidden in that little cave. We must check it out."

So I held his rifle and waited in the riverbed while he climbed a tree growing out of the bank to get high enough to see into the crack in the rock. I

145

stood there impatiently watching him climb higher and higher until he was opposite the crevice. Then he stuck his head into it and the next moment all hell broke loose!

A swarm of bees came out of the crack and attacked Bob. They stung him several times and in his mad panic to get away from his tiny tormentors, he fell out of the tree.

Fortunately he didn't injure himself seriously. He landed on the sand by my feet with a thud, but immediately jumped up and took off downriver to escape from the bees. I was ahead of him. Fortunately the tiny creatures didn't pursue us, but merely buzzed angrily around the entrance to their hive.

Tangling with bees was Bob's kind of luck.

Many months later, Bob was leading a night patrol down a kopje towards a kraal. He made his way slowly in an effort to be as quiet as possible. Then in the dark he stepped on a loose rock which caused him to fall heavily.

The rest of the patrol froze when they heard him fall with a grunt. Moments later it was dead quiet again and the second man in the patrol slowly inched forward to find out what had happened. When he reached Bob and bent over him, the injured man whispered in shock, "I've broken my leg!"

The guy said, "Aaah, bull man, lemme see!" He grabbed Bob's leg and wiggled it about until he was satisfied that it was indeed broken. Bob, of course, was in absolute agony, but somehow managed to prevent himself from screaming.

Then the third man in the patrol arrived and asked what was going on. In a whisper he was told, "Bob's broken his leg!"

He too reacted with a "Aaah, bull man, lemme see" and felt for Bob's leg so that he could wiggle it about to establish whether it was broken or not. After a short while of wiggling it about he too agreed that it was indeed broken.

The fourth and fifth men had their turn as well. According to Bob, they all without fail said, "Aaah, bull man, lemme see."

Each one also insisted on wiggling Bob's leg until they were satisfied that the bone had snapped.

Eventually and mercifully, the guys decided to abandon the patrol and called for a chopper casevac (casualty evacuation) on the radio. They were told there were no helicopters available, but that a truck would be sent to fetch Bob as soon as possible.

They slowly helped Bob down the hill and during the early hours of the morning a Bedford arrived with a medic. Bob was lifted onto the back of the truck where he lay down. By now, he was in even more agony and the bumpy road didn't help at all.

The medic eventually felt sorry for him and injected some morphine as they drove towards the hospital in Umtali.

When I visited him in hospital he told me, "Yeeouw, man that morphine is good stuff. There I was almost dying from the pain and then one shot of morphine later I was singing, "Roll out the barrel" at the top of my voice. I can now understand why people get hooked on drugs."

I wondered what was going to happen next to Bob, but rather him than me. I loved that guy and always looked forward to going into the bush with him. Not only was he a great buddy and a tremendous source of laughter, he also made me feel safe because he was the perfect decoy whenever bad things happened.

oooOooo

THE LAST WORD

Colonel Brown was full of bull, but he was a born leader. I think he may have been the youngest man ever to command our battalion. He had character too, perhaps even too much. I seem to recall seeing him with a huge civilian .45 calibre revolver strapped to his waist General Patton style. High ranking officers were like that. Although they weren't at the sharp end of the war as often as we were, they did perhaps like to display their machismo side as much as we did.

Our problem was that unlike them, where we were most of the time there were never any curvy girls around to see it. Just many lady baboons who spitefully chose to ignore us.

When the war first started we were a neat army. That was due to our British colonial roots. However, considering Rhodesia's rugged bush and especially the heat, it was a ridiculous way to dress.

As the war progressed our army evolved. We became an extremely shabby lot.

The focus of military life slipped away from shiny boots, sparkling buckles and berets and other such parade-like bulldust to whatever was comfortable and whatever helped to kill the enemy and helped to stop him killing us.

We became a well-oiled and deadly killing machine in exchange it seemed, for looking like a bunch of thieving pirates.

Most guys wore veldskoens (hide shoes) or black army-issue sneakers on their feet without socks. Almost everyone wore shorts. Some cut the sleeves off their camouflage shirts at the shoulder while others merely wore their army camouflage T-shirts or green army-issue vests. Although I preferred my camouflage cap, some guys wore camouflage net bandannas wrapped around their heads. And sensible guys didn't wear underpants either because it was cooler and more comfortable without them.

Wearing socks in the Rhodesian bush was an absolute no-no. Socks had too many enemies in that country. Spear grass, blackjacks and in the worst scenario, buffalo beans. Buffalo beans were the meanest plants because they cause a burning-itchy sensation, while speargrass seemed to be alive the way it can burrow right through your sock and into your skin.

Of course during the winter months the guys would dress more warmly, especially at night when you were lying on the ground in an ambush position. A few guys even wore pantyhose under their denim trousers when on an ambush.

I sometimes wondered about those guys.

Most troopies also stopped shaving when in the bush which resulted in what must have been the hairiest army in the world on a man-for-man basis.

When a soldier had been in the bush for a long time, he could eventually think of only one thing. We were young, we were fit and we were virile. Despite the army lacing our coffee with bluestone whenever we were back in base, we whittled away at our boredom on the mountains, in the valleys, next to streams, beside boulders and beneath trees with constant thoughts about our women.

I can't speak for the guys who wore pantyhose at night though.

All-night ambushes were very boring things. Imagine lying on your stomach in the dirt for eight or nine hours, not moving and not making a sound. It would have been fine if you could sleep, but of course that was not allowed because the enemy might walk into the killing zone at any time.

All you could do was wrestle with your thoughts.

You would lie there on the hard ground, uncomfortable as hell, and think about your cattle. Then, after a while and for some strange reason that cow in your mind would turn into a woman. You could fight against the thought and the woman might suddenly start growing horns or have an udder and a tail, but only for a brief moment before the curvy lady would return in all her glory.

You would be stunned by her soft shining hair and notice that her lips looked so inviting. Her face would be so pretty and in her eyes would be "that look" which of course, never failed to excite you.

You would imagine your hand on her breast, your fingers seeking her nipple and it responding to your touch. You would imagine stroking her soft warm belly and cupping her rounded bottom, lightly tickling her thighs, stroking her back and exploring ever closer to the triangular forest of joy.

Sometimes, especially when it was full moon, you might even imagine you got a whiff of her unique and delightful female aroma...

As you lay there thinking so deeply about these things, a hyena might call in the distance which would spoil it all by dragging your thoughts back to reality.

That was when you realised that if the enemy had arrived quietly in the killing zone moments before, you probably wouldn't even have known. At that point one might glance at your luminous watch and to your disappointment see only minutes had passed.

Before you knew it your mind would then return to where it had dwelled before.

There you would be – lying on a colourful quilt next to the Sabi River with the hippos frolicking in the pool behind you. You would be tickling her back and she would shiver with pleasure. You would glance at the crocodile lying on the island before noticing the tiny goose bumps on her upper arms and shoulders.

She would breathe ever more heavily and that was when you started hoping the stupid hyena would keep his big mouth shut.

Then when you heard the hyena's loud "whoo-oof" pierce the silence of the night yet again, you would curse him in your mind and at the same time be grateful that the enemy hadn't arrived at that crucial moment while only your body was ambushing them.

The point was during ambushes your mind would continually go home and there was nothing you could do about it. Those thoughts were dangerous because there was a war on.

Fortunately if the hyena didn't snap you out of your trance, your officer usually would by snoring so loudly it sounded like an elephant's tummy rumbling. I was most annoyed once when my snoring officer instantly transported my thoughts from the banks of the Sabi River to a darn hard piece of ground next to the Mazoe River. I decided to wake him up so that I could go back to the Sabi.

I felt around in the dark until I found a tiny stone and then bounced it off his head. He was quite annoyed so I politely whispered, "You were snoring!" His indignant reply, was so typical of an officer.

"How could I have been snoring? I wasn't even sleeping!"

That was the difference between officers and troopies. A troopie would merely have said, "Sorry."

I once told the Italian, Massimo Uglietti, about the cow turning into a woman and he said he had a similar problem. He told me that whenever he lay in an all night ambush and thought about his pigs, one of the fat sows would turn into his mother-in-law.

The closer we came to the end of our six-week spell in the bush, the more we thought about our women - and with tremendous anticipation.

We would ask each other, "What's the first thing you're going to do when you get home?"

The answer, accompanied by a lecherous smile, would invariably be something like, "Let's just say the second thing I'm going to do is take my boots off."

The soldiers of Charlie Company, after six long weeks in the bush, had reached that desperate stage.

However, just two days before they were due to return home, Colonel Brown told the Sergeant Major to fall the men in. Then Colonel Brown bluntly told them that they weren't going home, but would instead be staying in the bush for an additional two weeks.

Most of us were battle-hardened and extremely tough troops, but that didn't stop the odd tear from sliding down a cheek.

At that point the men hated their commander far more than they hated the hyena. The hyena shattered their dreams, the colonel shattered reality.

The troopies were devastated. The devastation quickly turned into rage, but it was a hopeless sort of anger. They were furious, but knew there was nothing they could do about the situation. Their morale sank to an all-time low.

Some sections were immediately dispatched on patrols and those that remained in the camp just sat around and moaned. They were so despondent that for once the thoughts of some turned from their women to planning the perfect murder – killed in crossfire. The soldiers certainly were cross.

I once heard that during an enemy mortar attack on Grand Reef aerodrome, two regular soldiers had completely ignored the incoming bombs and had gone looking for their own officer instead, with murder in mind. Fortunately for him they hadn't been able to find him in the dark.

Later the same day he'd given us the bad news, Colonel Brown strolled past two soldiers who were sitting sulking. As he walked by, one of the soldiers, at the top of his voice, asked his buddy, "What's the colour of shit?"

"Brown," was the answer.

oooOooo

SWEET DREAMS

Getting ready for a cross-border military operation was quite exciting. A bit like being in the dressing-room before an important rugby match. As sweet as stolen fruit in a way because you knew you were going into someone else's territory armed to the teeth and without a passport.

In your own country you were a soldier, but the moment you crossed over the border with a weapon you became a terrorist. The hunter became the hunted.

We had been patrolling in the Centenary area when we suddenly received orders to return to base as quickly as we could. When we arrived there, everything was already packed and we just climbed onto the back of the Bedford trucks and left. We wondered what was going on and asked the others, but no one knew.

We drove along the escarpment and then steeply down into the sweltering heat of the Zambezi Valley. We rode the trucks for many a dusty mile that day before eventually arriving at Mzungedzi Mission Station.

That place was something else. For some strange reason, I'm still nostalgic about it and want to return there for a visit before I die.

It was like having being taken out of Rhodesia and plonked down in Mexico. Red brick walls, cactus, dust, a few chickens and pigs running around and a genuine bell tower. Like the Mexicans in the movies, the guard in the bell tower had bandoliers of shiny brass bullets criss-crossing his chest.

The former mission station was the base of a Rhodesian African Rifles battalion known fondly as the RAR. They were a regular outfit consisting of African troops who all came from the same tribe. Their officers were white men. The RAR had fought in many places for decades, exotic-sounding places like Egypt, Malaya and Burma. They had a proud military heritage and we were proud of them as well.

I'd never worked with them, but I'd heard they were good soldiers.

I was lying lazily on my stretcher in the sun that afternoon when a sow and her half dozen piglets, who were fooling around in a tiny muddy pool under the water bowser, were startled by someone approaching. The fat sow bolted and ran over me and my stretcher. Before I could recover from the surprise of being trampled, the gang of little porkers also galloped over me and left me covered in mud. My buddies were amused. I wasn't.

We still didn't know what we were doing there, but late that afternoon the RAR Major briefed us.

He said, "Tomorrow morning you are flying into Mozambique." He tapped the map on the easel to show us where we were headed. "There is a chief in this area who is fence-sitting and we are going to flood the ground with troops in an effort to convince him he should side with us and not the enemy."

He also told us that there was a Frelimo policeman in the area and that we should try to find and arrest him. Apparently this copper knew a great deal about the terrorists.

Frelimo was the Mozambique Liberation Front which, after many years of war with the Portuguese, won the first democratic election and became the government.

We were also warned not to drink the river water unless we had boiled it or treated it with our chlorine tablets. Apparently there had been a recent cholera outbreak in the area.

At dawn the next morning, five helicopters landed at the base and 18 of us and two RAR soldiers clambered aboard.

As we flew north across the border towards the Zambezi River, I realised the major's idea of a "flood" and mine were somewhat different. Inserting 20 troops into an area about the size of Scotland wasn't my idea of a "flood" at all.

I noticed the guys weren't all that friendly towards the two RAR men at first, but that changed later.

We soon discovered that compared to them, we were a bunch of farmers with weapons. They were true professionals.

We were walking along in single file when a cobra crossed the path directly in front of the lead man. He staggered backwards which caused a chain-reaction.

We all stopped and stood where we were wondering what was happening at the front, but the two RAR guys went into immediate action. One shot off to the left and then dived down and rolled in behind the cover of a tree ready to shoot. The other did the same thing, but off to the right.

I'll never forget that place. It was the hottest place I've ever been to and I've been in the Namib Desert.

As we walked that first afternoon the guys started dropping from heat fatigue. I also dropped. I just had no energy and suddenly I felt dizzy. I had so little energy that I knew I wouldn't be able to take another step. I felt totally drained.

The guys put me in the shade and made me drink some salt tablets and plenty of water. After two or three hours I recovered.

Heat fatigue was serious stuff. Not only because it could kill you, but also because we were nowhere near a hospital. We were in another country – a hostile one. Wisely our officer decided "day patrols were out." We would walk at night.

We patrolled alongside the Mzungedzi River towards the mighty Zambezi and then after a few miles we moved further away from the river and eventually located the chief's kraal. We interrogated the old man a bit and he soon identified the Frelimo policeman whom we took prisoner.

I saw a sight in that strange kraal that will be in my mind forever. It was hellish hot and we parked ourselves under some trees which offered a bit of shade. I was sitting with my back against a tree facing the chief's hut. I noticed that the thatch roof of the untidy-looking huts hung well over the sides, no doubt as protection against the intense heat.

In front of me and in the shade around the hut, everyone was sitting motionless – and I mean everyone. It was more or less: man, dog, woman, rooster, youth, pig, child, another dog, turkey, another child, hen, another pig, another child, cat and so on.

I was sorry I hadn't brought my camera with.

It was tsetse fly area and those people were badly affected with the sleeping sickness carried by the flies. Several of them also had elephantitis disease. I saw a woman whose one leg was the size of her waist and there was an old man whose testicles were enormous. So big that whenever he wanted to move, which wasn't often, a *piccanin* (young boy) carried his nuts around for him.

It made me appreciate my own good health.

The Frelimo policeman certainly wasn't what I had expected. I wish the Scotland Yard guys could have seen him. He was dressed in rags and he badly needed a bath. We interrogated him, demanding that he hand his weapon over to us. At first he denied having a weapon, but we eventually managed to persuade him that it wouldn't be a good idea to lie and he reluctantly led us into the bush.

Of course I expected him to hand over an almost new Russian AK-47 assault rifle, but he dug an ancient Tower musket out from under a pile of leaves! Mozambique was full of surprises.

We were all slightly mystified to discover that the locals referred to us as the "Ma-British." I wondered if Harold Wilson, who was the Prime Minister of Britain at the time, would have approved of "his troops" cross border raid? Rhodesia had declared unilateral independence from Britain, one of the factors which led to the bush war.

The next day a chopper fetched our policeman prisoner and a day later, after having been interrogated, he was returned to us again. He was now handcuffed. We were told he had agreed to lead us to the terrorist camp in the area and that we should attack it immediately.

Our officer's plan was to split us into two groups. We would attack in an "L" formation. I was to lead the attack (the bottom part of the L) and the other section would act as a stop-group on our left.

I was nervous because we didn't know how many of the enemy to expect inside that camp. I comforted myself by reasoning that the RAR commander wouldn't expect us to attack vast numbers of the enemy. However, I also knew that the Rhodesian Army throughout the war, never thought twice about attacking ten times their own number.

The guy leading the stop group section on my left was a rugby player like myself and I had great respect for him simply because he was a huge man who had played at provincial level. It proved to be a mistake on my part.

We moved through extremely dense bush with our prisoner, scanning the area in front of us continually as best we could. Suddenly we broke through the bush into a cleared area. We stopped with our fingers on the triggers of our rifles ready to open up, and searched for targets ahead of us. There were none.

It was definitely the terrorist camp because we could see the flattened grass where they had slept. We also saw where they had made their cooking fires.

I felt the ashes and they were cold. The terrorists had left quite a while ago. I had mixed feelings; in a way I was relieved and in a way I was disappointed too.

I reasoned that someone in the chief's kraal had snuck out and warned them that the Ma-British had arrived.

When we realised there wasn't going to be a battle, we shouted to the stop-group guys on our left to move into the enemy camp. They didn't answer because they weren't there. Later when we found them quite some distance away, the section commander told us they had lost their direction a bit in the dense bush and had gone way too far left.

We left it at that, but in my heart I knew he hadn't told us the truth. The truth was that he was a coward. Our officer agreed with me and I suspect something was written into that man's military record.

In the end this didn't matter because years later everyone started burning army records the moment it became known Robert Mugabe was the new leader of the country.

We moved away from the camp and when the sun started setting, we stopped and had some tea and a meal. When it was properly dark, we grabbed our rifles and gear and moved away to find a place to sleep.

We never bedded down in the same place where we were at dusk. We had been warned the chances were good that the enemy would mortar us at night. We would simply wait until dark, walk half a mile or so in any direction and bed down in all round defensive mode.

That night I slept well because I was tired and maybe the tension of the day also had something to do with it.

I woke to laughter around me the next morning. I opened my eyes to find my buddies gathered around me chuckling away and wondered what was going on? Dave Brown asked me whether I had enjoyed sweet dreams that night, but I didn't have a clue what he was talking about?

I soon found out. In the black of the night I had plonked my body down lengthways exactly on top of a grave. The granite rock behind my head turned out to be the tombstone.

After ten days inside Mozambique without having taken our boots off, we were more than ready to head home for a shower and a cold beer.

While the officer radioed base asking for the choppers to fetch us, I thought of that flight home because I had been on similar ones. After not having washed for so long in that heat we smelled like a bunch of skunks, but we all stank so it didn't bother us much. I knew though that the sweet-smelling helicopter pilots would be flying with their heads hanging out of their doorless aircraft to get some fresh air. It would be nice revenge for all the pranks the Blue Jobs pulled on us.

It was not to be though. We were simply told, "The choppers are not available, so just walk back." The Blue Jobs were always one step ahead of us.

I can't remember how far it was, probably 70 miles or more? We started walking at about two that afternoon and we walked through the night and for part of the next morning. We stopped only once for about an hour when the Vumba farmer Paddy Murphy collapsed.

He was a little guy and was carrying the machine-gun. After he had recovered several of us offered to help him with the big gun, but he politely refused all our offers. Paddy was small, but he had a big heart and was as tough as teak.

When daylight came we looked around for landmarks to establish exactly where we were, but the Zambezi Valley floor there was so flat that it was difficult to pinpoint our position. We studied the Portuguese map we had been given and saw a hill clearly marked near where we thought we were. We searched all around for that wee hill, but saw nothing.

Then someone put two and two together. We discovered that the banana plantation directly in front of us and which was about 10 inches higher than the surrounding countryside was the so-called hill on the Portuguese map. After raiding the plantation like a troop of marauding baboons, we crossed the border.

When we radioed our position back to base, they told us the choppers were on their way and we should stay where we were.

The pilots all flew with their heads cocked to the right. Well into the slipstream.

oooOooo

DEAR ALAN

There were four of us manning the observation point on top of the mountain.

It was an easy job. All we had to do was take turns scanning the surrounding countryside with powerful binoculars for terrorists. If we saw any terrorists or anything suspicious we had to radio the Fire Force.

Although it was a nice change from walking, we soon became very bored.

On the fourth day when we started complaining about our boredom Alan Richardson did an evil thing. He pulled an unopened letter from his pack and gleefully said, "This is just what I've been waiting for. You guys are bored stiff and here in my hand I have a letter from my wife that I've been saving for an occasion like this."

Obviously he wanted to make us envious and he succeeded, but I knew I would never be able to keep a letter unopened for days as he'd done. Especially not during that particular bush trip. I'd received several letters from my wife and each time, among other news I'd read something like, "Another four cows died this week."

That was the year of the big drought in Manicaland and I'd already started wondering whether there would be any cattle left on my land when I eventually made it home?

Then Alan started reading his letter as we watched.

Suddenly he said, "Oh, no!"

I thought then he had heard his cattle were also dying, but after another "Oh, no!" and a "Shit!" he started explaining what his letter was about.

"My wife has left me, guys! She's gone back to the UK."

When I heard that I felt really sorry for him and I'm sure the other two guys did as well. I couldn't understand how a woman could do that to a guy. Leave him sure, but don't wait until he's on top of a mountain in the back of beyond before letting him know. Tell him face to face.

I sort of felt she'd now made her problem ours.

We didn't know what to say to Alan. What do you say to a man who has just found out his wife has gone? The thought crossed my mind that maybe we should take his weapon away from him just in case...

Alan started pacing up and down still reading the letter. "She's taken the kids with her," he said.

"Oh, no," we groaned in sympathy.

"It's OK guys, they were her kids from a previous marriage. I was fond of them, but it's OK."

He started reading the second page when I said, "Alan, I'll radio base and tell them you urgently need some compassionate leave. I can also arrange for you to speak to skypilot (the padre's code name) if you want..."

"Wait, sarge, let me finish this letter."

He continued pacing up and down while we exchanged worried glances.

Then he said, "Sarge, please radio and try and get me off this mountain. I've got to get back home to find out whether she took my antique furniture with her."

"Shit," I said, as I thought, no wonder she left him.

oooOooo

171

INTRODUCTION TO THE M962

Whenever we were called up for six-week bush stints, we would always train on a range somewhere for two or three days before heading for an operational area. This was to enable the men to zero in their rifles and also to introduce them to new weapons and strategies.

We didn't often receive new weapons, but I do recall the day they told us our old Second World War Mills hand grenades were to be replaced by the American M-962 grenade.

We sat there in the sun in a half circle as the instructor explained everything about the new grenade. Using it was no different to the Mills, you just pulled the pin out and tossed the grenade. The M-962 didn't have a base plug though, to get the detonator out you had to unscrew the top of the grenade, which meant that the detonator, safety

173

pin and handle all came away from the metal and explosive part. It wasn't necessary to ever clean the grenade and the only reason why you would ever unscrew the top would be if you wanted to prepare a grenade "necklace" by stringing several grenades together with cortex fuse.

Only a few of us, who had done the explosives course, knew how to do that.

Everything else about the M-962 was basic stuff like on hard ground it has a killing range of 100 yards and so on.

When he had completed his lecture, the instructor said, "Any questions?"

That was when my cousin Ben asked, "What if it doesn't explode?"

I froze, when he asked because I knew that was exactly the type of question instructors hated. They knew we often asked questions like that not because we were interested in the answers, but because we merely wanted to waste time.

It was nice sitting there smoking in the sun and we knew that we would be getting all sweaty skirmishing and leopard-crawling in the dust and thorns once the grenade session was over.

The instructor had a little fit and didn't even answer the question properly.

"Fourteen million of these grenades were thrown in Vietnam and never, not even once, did one fail to explode," he barked, glaring at Ben as though he was a moron.

Then we were each allowed to toss one live grenade into the dense bush in front of us.

Nothing unusual happened until my cousin tossed his grenade.

It was a good throw, but there was no bang.

He turned from where he was lying on his belly and looked at the instructor before saying, "How many grenades did they throw in Vietnam?"

The instructor had a second little fit. He was quite sure now that my dear cousin was trying to take the Mickey out of him. His face became quite red and he accusingly shouted, "You didn't pull the pin out, you retarded soldier, you!"

My cuz was always one-up on that guy, he held up his left hand and there dangling from his fingers was a grenade pin.

"Oh yes, what's this then Staff Sergeant?"

Of course our entire platoon was watching and when they saw the pin everyone burst out laughing.

I thought it was quite uncanny that one man asks what happens if the grenade doesn't explode and then that same man's grenade fails.

The instructor didn't back off from the confrontation yet. He ordered Ben to crawl into the bush and find his grenade. My cousin, to his credit, didn't back off either.

"No," he answered, "You said they always go off, so you go and find it."

There can't be many jobs worse than crawling around in dense bush looking for a live pinless grenade that could explode at any moment and if it didn't go bang and you found it, you still had to blow it up by gently packing plastic explosive against it. Very gently.

Because of what he'd said about Vietnam, the instructor knew he had to do it. He asked my cousin where he had thrown it and then slowly and carefully crawled forward into the bush to find the now-dangerous bomb.

We were happy because we were in for a much longer than planned smoke in the sun.

The instructor disappeared slowly into the bush while we puffed away. After a long time, my cousin shouted to him, "Have you found it, Staff?"

"No."

"Ok, hang on, I'll come and help you," my cousin said.

I suspect he remembered exactly where he had tossed the grenade because he and the instructor soon found it and together they packed explosives onto it and then detonated it from a safe distance. The Rhodesian war just wasn't like Vietnam.

oooOooo

WALKING UNDER THE MOON

After many years of war the Rhodesian Army started employing different tactics. We started to patrol at night instead of during the day. It made sense because previously it seemed we always moved around during the day, while the enemy always seemed to move at night.

I'm a man who ate more than my fair share of carrots for sure. I used to pluck them out of the soil in our vegetable garden, wash them under the tap and then munch them, yet I had great difficulty seeing properly at night. My night blindness nearly got me into trouble a couple of times and once it did.

I recall a night patrol in the Hot Springs area when I was leading a patrol. I suddenly saw this white stuff in front of me and so I stopped in an effort to find out what it was. I stared at the white stuff for a few moments and then the second man in the patrol came up to me and asked why I had stopped?

Before I could answer him, he said, "Don't move, take a step back!"

He might have saved my life because I was standing right on the edge of a high river bank. It was a dry river and the white stuff I could see was river sand roughly 25 feet below me.

Some months later, whilst leading a night patrol near the Mozambique border east of Chisumbanje, I repeatedly walked into scrub bush. Eventually Johan de Beer came to my rescue. He said, "You can't see at night sarge, let me take the lead."

I was grateful because I knew sooner or later I was going to be jabbed in the eye.

We continued our patrol and not five minutes later Johan suddenly stopped in front of me. We all stopped and listened in silence behind him and then after a short while I moved forward and asked, "What's wrong Johan?"

"There's a puffadder lying in the path in front of me."

I looked carefully and sure enough, there the poisonous snake was with a body thicker than my arm lying with its head raised - ready to strike. Johan stuck his FN barrel under the snake and flipped it sideways into the bush and we continued on our patrol.

Had I still been leading the men I would have stepped on the snake for sure and would have been bitten. I had no doubt about that.

Our entire company was once ordered to do a "cordon and search" on a village suspected of harbouring terrorists. The plan was to march in at night from miles away and surround the village during the early hours of the morning and then to move in at first light.

We marched in and surrounded the village and we were all moving in just a bit to tighten the cordon to the point where we were close enough to see each other. At that stage I couldn't see anyone, but I could hear a man on my left and another on my right. I could hear them stumbling forward in the dark.

I decided to move about ten paces closer. I took three steps and then suddenly felt myself falling! It all happened very quickly and the next moment I landed in ice cold water with an almighty splash. My rifle barrel pegged deeply into the mud at the bottom of the river. I plucked it out and surfaced and as my head broke clear of the water I heard a splash not two yards away!

My mind said "crocodile" and I took off in a mad silent panic. Within seconds I had crossed the water and scrambled to the top of the far bank. As I sat there breathing heavily I could hear a guy laughing to my left and another laughing to my right.

I felt like a real fool, but couldn't help laughing as well.

Afterwards I decided that it probably hadn't been a "flatdog" that had caused the splash next to me. Far more likely my falling into the river had disturbed a leguaan (a huge type of lizard) who had then dived into the water for safety.

A guy called Anthony who I used to play rugby with, had a much closer shave during a night patrol. They were patrolling during a very dark night when they walked slap-bang into a terrorist patrol!

He told me it was absolute chaos. Everyone was shooting and running around in the thick bush without really knowing who they were shooting at. Anthony said that when the shooting started he saw Sadza, one of his Shona rifleman, on his righthand side. He grabbed Sadza's shoulder and shouted "Get down, get down!"

The man replied, "No let's go," and had then run off into the bush.

After a while when everything had calmed down again, Anthony realised he had grabbed and had a conversation with a terrorist!

He knew that for sure because Sadza was the only Shona soldier in his patrol and Sadza was lying on his left, not right and he was quite dead.

ooooOoooo

WATER

If you asked an instructor what was inside a grenade he would answer, "square ball bearings." It was that kind of an army.

Take the time when many patrols and spotter planes were combing the Zambezi Valley for terrorists and could find none despite much evidence that they were infiltrating on a regular basis. Some high ranking officer decided they were probably sneaking across the valley at night and hiding in the majestic and rugged Mavuradonna Mountains while we searched the valley in vain.

He decided the logical thing to do was to send many patrols to search those mountains. Not a bad idea at all, but typical of officers who sit in base camps drinking beer and making plans, he decided the choppers should take us down to the valley floor and we should then climb back up to the top of the Great African Plateau searching for the enemy as we go.

To me it was a "square ball bearing" plan because we were already on top of the mountain. We could've walked down and the choppers could've fetched us at the bottom.

Maybe the fact that he wasn't the one who was going to do the climbing had something to do with it?

It was cool on top of the plateau and we were shocked at the difference in temperature when we arrived on the valley floor. Down there it was hellish hot.

There were four of us and we nonchalantly started climbing the steep mountain. Our nonchalance only lasted a few minutes though.

We suddenly realised we had one hell of a climb ahead of us and already we were sweating profusely in that heat and from the effort of dragging our bodies and gear up. The mountain was so steep that we had to take short rests after every eight or nine steps. Our legs went numb from the strain and resting them for half a minute or so seemed to allow them to recover.

We climbed and climbed and took little sips from our water bottles until after a couple of hours we had no water left. None of us were too worried about that because we felt we were near the top.

As we struggled up that mountain, I wondered whether anyone had ever been where we were? No sane person would attempt that climb without a very good reason. We saw an interesting thing during our climb and we were unsure what it was. It was a round ball of fluff with a tiny head and eyes in the centre!

We took a short rest and studied the insect. It didn't appear to be able to walk, but would move around by being blown by the slightest breeze. One of the guys said he knew an insect expert at the University of Rhodesia and would find out whether or not we had discovered something new.

Some months later he told us the insect we had seen was a spider. Quite a rare one, but not undiscovered.

The massive mountain proved to be extremely misleading. One could see the top just ahead of you and then when you reached that spot, there would be another top just ahead.

We climbed higher and higher over many "tops" until I thought we would never reach the crest.

I became so thirsty that eventually all I could think of was water. My tongue started swelling and felt thick in my dry mouth and I knew that if we didn't find water soon we would all die on that mountain. Although no one said so, I think the others knew as well.

It was frightening.

All those years in "the sticks" I had wondered whether there was a bullet with my name on it and never once did it cross my mind that I might die of thirst. Neither could we call for help because we couldn't raise anyone on the radio. I think it was because we were on the side of the mountain and the radio relay station was on top?

I'd been really thirsty in the bush once before, but we'd found a tiny pool of slimy, dirty water with a smelly jackal carcass floating in it. We had slowly shoved the stinking jackal's body to the far side of the pool with a stick before quenching our thirst on the near side.

I was way past the stage of worrying about drinking rotten water. Any form of moisture would do.

We were constantly looking around us for signs of water and then I glanced up and saw the Rhodesian sky was as blue as ever and there was only one miserable little cloud in the distance.

Extremely desperate now, I started praying and asking the Lord for water.

Later and after many more silent prayers, I looked skyward again and saw that the cloud had blown a bit closer to where we were!

That boosted my faith tremendously and I prayed even harder.

Then just when we were in the shadow of that tiny cloud it started raining...

It didn't rain much. Just enough for each of us to quench our thirst and fill our water bottles by holding them against the side of a boulder thereby allowing the water to trickle in. It struck me as quite uncanny that all four of us just managed to fill our bottles exactly to the brim before there was no more water.

To me, that was further proof that God had indeed answered my prayers.

I then felt that I could not keep my mouth shut. I had to give the glory to God.

So I said, "Guys, I want to tell you the rain wasn't coincidence, I prayed for it and God sent it. We have to be grateful to the Lord Jesus. He saved us."

Petrus Coetzee laughed and said, "Don't for a moment think you were the only one praying see."

John Baker added "I also prayed."

Guy Shaw spoilt the golden moment by saying, "Crap man, we were just lucky."

I didn't say anything to him nor did the others. I just felt very sorry for him.

About thirty years later I read in the paper that he had been arrested and was in a Zimbabwean prison after being caught dealing in illegal gold.

oooOooo

PLOP

When I first went into the army, I had no knowledge about how to keep myself dry when it rained. I soon learnt though, I had to otherwise I would have spent many miserable days and nights totally drenched.

In Scotland when it drizzles the people say "it's bucketing down" and when they hear a single clap of thunder at night, which seems to be rare in Scotland, they will talk about the electrical storm the next morning.

Whenever I heard them talking like that I would just smile because I wondered what they would say if they experienced an African storm? Africa has many far more vicious storms several times during a single rainy season. Many people get killed by lightning each year as well.

If we thought it was going to rain, we would erect little shelters between two trees with two joined ponchos using string or nylon cord. Those little tents were called bivvies. If the bivvy was erected on slightly sloping ground we would dig shallow furrows to divert the water around the bivvy-tent instead of through it.

It never ceased to amaze me that one could stay dry under such a flimsy thing, but we did. Well most of the time anyway.

I recall Dave Flower and myself lying in a bivvy in the Matopos while it rained cats and dogs. Outside it was as wet as can be, but inside it was bone dry. Then out of sheer boredom I touched the bivvy above me with a finger.

A short while later, a drop of cold water landed on my nose! I looked carefully and then suspected it had leaked where I had touched the bivvy. I touched another spot just to make sure and sure enough, not long after that it started leaking there as well.

"Dave," I said, "Don't touch the bivvy see, I did and now it is leaking where I touched it."

"Rubbish," he answered and touched the bivvy above himself.

We lay there staring at the spot and then after a short while – plop! The drop of water landed on his forehead. In the meantime there had been several more plops on me from the spots I had touched.

Then several years later, we were operating on the border in the lowveld near Chisumbanje when cyclone Domoina hovered in the Mozambique channel causing heavy rainfall in Manicaland and other parts of Rhodesia. It rained so hard and so often that the place started flooding.

Helicopters had to rescue people off the roof at the Lion and Elephant Motel and every now and again there was a cloudburst somewhere. Thinking back now, it seemed to rain almost daily for about six weeks while we were in the bush.

Of course it didn't rain continuously. The sun would come out for a few hours and then the dark clouds would gather and the rain would come down again. We tried to stay dry, but it was impossible.

In particular, I recall one night we were sleeping on the ground in the bush when suddenly and without warning, it started raining really hard. We were totally drenched within seconds and saw no point in trying to find shelter somewhere. We also knew there was no shelter anywhere near us.

Besides we were really tired and just wanted to sleep. So sleep we did.

I must have woken up and drifted back to sleep a thousand times that night. The next morning I found I was sleeping in a couple of inches of water.

Sometimes I think it was only because we were so fit that we didn't end up developing pneumonia. I don't think any of us even caught a cold.

Our clothes were permanently damp which caused other problems. Maggot flies laid their eggs on some of us without us even knowing. Neither did we know about it when the tiny worms hatched and burrowed into our flesh.

We only found out when we felt pain and then it was too late. The little bastards would already be deep inside your flesh. We all knew what to do. Normally one smears a little bit of Vaseline over the top which causes the worm to move towards the surface of your skin in an effort to get some air. Then you squeeze it out. We didn't have any Vaseline so we used army issue margarine instead.

That did the trick too, but it was quite painful squeezing the little worms out and after they were removed there was always a tiny hole in your flesh.

After a heavy bout of maggots, we decided we had to make a plan to stay dry.

One night as we bedded down, the dark clouds blew over again and we hastily packed up our gear and went looking for shelter. Just when it started raining we spotted a lone hut and ran for it.

We didn't knock on the door and ask to be let in. We just knocked the flimsy door open and burst in. It wasn't because we intended to be rude, nor because it had started raining, but because there was a chance that an armed terrorist could be sheltering inside there as well and if that was the case we wanted to surprise him or them.

In the candlelight we saw two men and a woman lying close together on the floor under a blanket. The lady was in the middle. Judging by how they tried to cover themselves with the only blanket they had, it was obvious they were all naked.

After satisfying ourselves that it was safe inside that hut, we apologised for disturbing them and explained that we were merely trying to stay dry.

Shame, they looked quite startled and who can blame them? Four heavily armed bearded dirty soldiers suddenly appear on the scene and spoil their fun as well. They seemed a bit embarrassed so we joked about their predicament and in typical African fashion they laughed as much as we did.

I imagine someone from the UK in a similar position would have been reaching for the phone to get hold of a lawyer. Africa and Africans are very different.

We joked about how rich and special the woman must be to have two husbands which had them all laughing hysterically because in Africa during those days a woman was nothing. It was always the rich men who had many wives and never the other way around.

That was when the one guy explained that the woman was his wife.

"Your wife? Why then do you allow this naked man to sleep so close to her."

He laughed again and said, "He's my brother, it's okay."

We left it at that. I never did fully understand them and I knew any further questions would just puzzle me more.

We asked them to move up and went to sleep beside them.

It was so nice to lie inside that wood smoke-smelling hut and stay bone dry while it poured outside all night. The next morning we gave them a few tins of beef goulash and creamy chicken as a thank you gift. They were so grateful that we knew we could book into that "hotel" whenever we liked.

After our one dry night we decided we would in future move closer to huts whenever it looked as though a storm was brewing.

Despite our plans, we never slept inside a hut again.

We made our way back to base for a day's rest and learnt that we weren't the only ones hiding from Domoina inside huts. Everyone was doing it in an effort to stay dry and maggot-free.

Then a radio message made everyone decide that getting wet and having maggots burrow into your flesh was preferable to sleeping inside huts.

Jason Morris sent the message of doom.

"21 this is 21 Delta, do you read over?"

"21 Delta, 21 – reading you fives over."

"Roger 21, we are in deep trouble at this time. We spent last night sheltering inside a hut and now we are covered in lice over."

"Roger 21 Delta, where are you over?

"We are only about 500 yards from the camp and will be coming in shortly over."

"Negative 21 Delta, I repeat negative. Stay where you are. Do not move into camp, I say again, do not enter the camp. I'll send the medic to sort you out. Say goodbye to your hair and beards while you wait. Over and out."

Lice or maggots? Quite a choice.

oooOooo

FAIR SWAP

The men were exhausted, but happy they were all still alive. The bodies of the terrorists they had killed lay across from where they sat with their backs leaning against trees. Now that the battle was over, they smoked and chatted about what had happened as they waited for the helicopters to arrive.

Then Trooper Roberts rose and slowly walked over to where the bodies lay. The others stopped talking and wondered what he intended to do? They had already searched the dead terrorists...

Trooper Roberts stopped at the feet of one stiff bloated corpse and then slowly sat down. This made his comrades even more curious.

He carefully put the soles of his battered boots up against the terrorist's boots.

Then he started removing his boots followed by those of the dead man.

He smiled broadly as he walked away wearing his brand-new Russian boots.

oooOooo

FRIENDS

When I think back now I don't dwell on the hardships and the horror of war. I like to remember the good times and my buddies. It appears to be human nature to unite against a common enemy, although there are often exceptions as well. We became close friends, united I guess, against the enemy and when the enemy wasn't around probably against the officers.

Friends were plenty in the army and enemies few, although there were some.

I will remember the ones that fell for as long as I live. I miss them even now after so many years. Friends like Bruce, Ivan, Billy, Charles, Clippie and Tim...

I like to think the big German was one of my pals. He had been a professional hunter in Mozambique until the Portuguese quit their colony. He could tell some really good stories about taking the legendary actor, John Wayne, and the first man on the moon, Neil Armstrong out on safari.

They were probably just jealous of him, but one or two guys didn't believe the big German's stories. I had no reason not to believe him and besides I remembered my mother-in-law meeting Neil Armstrong in a shop in the Mozambican coastal city of Beira when we were on holiday there.

What happened was that mom strolled into a shop and this man came up to her and introduced himself saying, "I'm Neil Armstrong."

Mom replied, "Yeah sure and I'm the Queen Mother."

My mother-in-law is like that.

Then mom looked around and noticed the entire shop had been decorated to look like a space ship!

Beira during the sixties wasn't your run-of-the-mill city. Strange things happened there. I recall my wife and I looking at baboons in a private zoo when something rubbed against my leg. It was a young lion the size of a really big dog. I was horrified, but the zoo owner tried unsuccessfully to reassure me that the lion was tame and didn't need to be in a cage.

I heard that after a long battle in the Honde Valley, a long line of infantry troops were walking along a path flanked by dense bush on both sides. Suddenly the guys heard a shot behind them and dived for cover. However there were no further shots.

What had happened was that a terrorist had hidden right next to the path and everyone had strolled right past him without spotting him. Then the last man, the big German, had seen and shot the terrorist from the hip. To me that just proved he was what he said he was – a professional hunter.

Unlike everyone else, he didn't look at the bush. He looked through it.

ooooOoooo

ANIMALS

Surprisingly animals gave us soldiers who were constantly in the bush few problems. There were exceptions though. Charlie Scott was dragged out of his sleeping bag by a hyena one night.

Of course we should always have posted a guard at night, but were still young and foolish so often we all just went to sleep and hoped for the best. Charlie said, that was what they had done the night he was attacked.

The hyena had simply sneaked up to the four sleeping men and grabbed his head in its powerful jaws. The smelly animal had then dragged him out of his sleeping bag before he could scream. When he eventually managed to yell, the hyena dropped him and ran off. Charlie survived the attack, but the hyena had scalped him.

He was very lucky to survive, hyenas are known

to have extremely powerful jaws and can crunch thick bones as though they are macaroni sticks.

Our chopper pilots on occasion chased elephant with their aircraft. They were safe because they could hover outside the irate elephants' reach. It was a bad idea though. Over time some of the elephant which had been buzzed by helicopters learnt to hate the aircraft. Whenever they heard a chopper some of the more ill-tempered jumbo would head towards it.

That meant troops would have to run for their lives just after being dropped in the bush while the chopper crew were safe in the air on their way back to base.

I heard of one section of men who had to run away from a charging elephant the minute their feet touched the ground. The troops had spotted the elephant coming and so they immediately took to their heels. The helicopter gunner realised they had left in such a hurry that they had forgotten their TR28 radio, so he leaned over and gently dropped the radio in the grass before urgently shouting "Go-go-go" to the pilot.

The troops had run away so quickly they were under the impression that the radio was still safely inside the aircraft. They felt they didn't really have a choice, they would just have to complete their patrol without communications. They had their maps and they knew where their pick-up point was so they just continued on their merry way.

Three days later back in camp, their commander wanted to know why they had failed to communicate with him? They explained what had happened and then the aircrew were called in and asked where the very expensive radio was?

In the end they had to fly back to where the men had been dropped and found the radio still lying in the grass, none the worse for wear.

The foreigner, David Marshall from Liverpool, had a strange experience one dark night. He was lying in ambush when suddenly he felt something land on his back from the tree above. He froze and felt the "thing" moving up his back towards his head. He felt it crawl up his neck and onto the cap on his head. He could also feel something on his bum.

That was when he whispered out of the side of his mouth to Leon van Vuuren on his left, "Leon! There's something on me, what is it?"

Leon lifted himself up onto his elbows, looked carefully and said, "It's a snake, don't move I'll get my bayonet."

The Liverpudlian thought about Leon's words for a moment. Bayonet? Then leapt up with a yell and ran a few paces away.

Afterwards he explained to us that he hadn't been all that concerned about the snake, but thought Leon was going to stab the snake with his bayonet! Of course that hadn't been Leon's intention at all, he merely wanted to use his bayonet to flick the snake off David.

One night four of us camped near Sidindi Island on the Zambezi River. We made a roaring fire because we had seen fresh lion tracks not a hundred yards away. We cooked a meal, ate it and chatted for a long time whilst enjoying a couple of shots of whisky. Subsequently by the time we were ready to sleep, the fire was no more. Just some glowing coals.

Of course we could've searched for and fetched more firewood, but who was going to volunteer for that knowing there might be a lion lurking nearby?

Instead we crawled into our sleeping bags and settled down for the night. No guard either.

It was an exceptionally dark night.

Just before anyone managed to fall asleep we heard a strange noise. A crunching sound.

"Did you hear that?"

"Yes."

"What is it?"

"Don't know."

We listened carefully and realised whatever it was - it was close. Not close enough to see though. If only we had a powerful torch.

To me, it sounded just like a cow grazing? The crunching sound was grass being ripped I thought. That was crazy though. There were no cows around, we were in a massive game reserve? So it wasn't a cow. Therefore it must be an antelope of some kind, but that was also a crazy thought. No kudu, eland, waterbuck, impala or whatever would come and feed right next to humans?

Maybe the antelope is rabid, I thought, but then dismissed the thought knowing a rabid animal wasn't going to calmly graze.

One of the guys then tossed an empty tin in the direction where the crunching sound was coming from. The crunching stopped. Dead silence.

After only about 10 seconds of silence we heard "crunch, crunch!"

We decided whatever it was, it certainly wasn't a vegetarian lion and we didn't mind sleeping next to an antelope even if it was a noisy one. So we tried to sleep yet again.

Then after a while the Greek, Marco Mallachias said, "Can you guys sleep?"

"No."

"I wish that fucking animal would get lost."

"Let's shoot it."

I listened carefully and then aimed in the direction of the sound. Bang!

Dead silence.

Ten seconds later..."Crunch, crunch."

What the hell was wrong with this animal? Stone deaf or what?

We then surrendered and slept like dead men.

At dawn we investigated and soon saw the tracks of a lone hippo only about 15 paces away from where we had slept. I went cold. Not many people know hippo are extremely dangerous animals, perhaps the most dangerous judging by the number of people they kill in Africa each year. Male hippos weigh up to 5 000 lbs and females are slightly less obese.

"Our" hippo had chosen to ignore us, but I knew we'd been extremely lucky that I hadn't wounded it. Imagine tangling with a hippo in the dark.

oooOooo

MONEY TALKS

A Special Air Services (SAS) friend of mine once told me they captured a lone terrorist in the Zambezi Valley. Their prisoner had been in a bad way. He hadn't only been starving, but had also been desperate enough to drink his own urine. The Zambezi Valley can be a harsh place.

They had interrogated their prisoner who had told them he hadn't been alone. He said about 24 hours earlier his mate had left him under a tree to die.

Then he said something which excited the SAS men. He told them the man who had escaped was a terrorist paymaster and that he had a great deal of cash on him.

Feeling sorry for their prisoner, they gave him water and a tin of corned beef. Not long after eating the man died. Apparently the meal killed him.

In the meantime, an SAS man had found the other terrorist's tracks and the men took to the trail with more zest than usual. In fact they were almost trotting after their quarry.

They tracked that man for days and were sure they were catching up to him at quite a rate. After a few days and after seeing on the map how much ground they had covered, their commander spoke to them on the radio.

He said, "Guys, you've done a great job and must be dead-beat now, so I'm going to send a chopper with fresh troops to take over from you."

The message horrified the guys and they quickly replied, "Negative, negative don't send replacement troops, we aren't tired at all and want to continue."

They tracked the wealthy terrorist right across the Zambezi Valley and deep into Zambia where they eventually lost the tracks...

oooOooo

CRACK SHOT

It made my day when I qualified as a marksman with the FN 7,62 mm assault rifle but it didn't really surprise me. My late father, whose passion in life had been hunting, had taught me to shoot before my arms were strong enough to hold a rifle. He would hold the rifle while I aimed and pulled the trigger.

While I was still a boy a guy called Sabudu, who I loved and who was our gardener, also helped me improve my shooting. After reading about William Tell, I asked him to place an empty jam tin on his head so that I could shoot it off. He readily agreed. Maybe the fact that he smoked marijuana all day had something to do with his willingness to help?

I shot empty cans off the old geezer's head with my Brno .22 rifle many times until one day my mom caught me at it. She threatened to wallop me

213

within an inch of my life if she ever saw me doing it again.

Sabudu was a bit upset when he realised, after a while, that the two of us were no longer making an effort to improve my markmanship. He thought I was angry with him. He was rather a strange man, his weekly working hours ended at noon on a Saturday and I always smiled when I heard him digging in mom's garden early on a Sunday morning. She would chase him home, but you could be sure he would come to work again the following Sunday morning.

My brother taught me an even neater shooting trick. We would ambush the women as they walked back from the river. We would shoot the water-filled clay pots they were balancing on their heads.

Fact is, we grew up hunting. My brother, who is older than me, even managed to get me to sign a hunting concession in my own blood. We split our parents' farm up into hunting areas and neither of us were allowed to hunt in the other's territory. Of course when he wasn't around I poached, but I'm sure he did the same when I was away.

I guess we were quite serious kids. My brother and I and two cousins and a friend once tried to derail the train on our farm. We were little guys then and quite innocent. We just wanted to watch the train crash.

My one cousin was a genius. It was his idea and when he tried to sell it to us we were keen, but didn't have a clue as to how we were going to budge the train.

"Easy as pie," he said. "We all just crap on the railway line and the train will slip off the rails."

So five little boys took their shorts off and parked little coils all over the railway line. Then we hid in some bushes nearby until someone enquired, "What if the train falls on us?"

We moved further away, but to our disappointment the train just roared past.

During one of bush camps with 4th Battalion, our Major split the platoon into two teams for a shooting competition. He had placed a long line of empty beer bottle targets on the far bank of the river where we were camped. If you hit a bottle you scored a point for your team and you were allowed to continue shooting. If you missed, you were history.

Most guys missed. A few would hit a bottle and then miss the second shot. When it was my turn I wiped out all the remaining bottles. I think there were seven of them.

As I lowered my rifle, Derek Murray raised an arm and pointed into the distance asking, "Can you hit that fly over there?"

"Which eye do you want me to shoot him in?" I asked.

Pride always comes before a fall. I fell really hard.

Instead of being rewarded I was punished. The major took my FN away and gave me a MAG 7,62 mm machine gun. Of course I protested, but he said, "The best shot must have the machine gun and I don't want to hear another word about this."

Now the major and I were farming neighbours and friends. We often hunted guineafowls, pheasants and partridges together using his two pointer dogs and 12-bore shotguns. I had also given him permission to shoot birds on my land whenever he wanted to.

I carried that machine gun over mountains and through valleys for the last 14 days of that camp and lost ten percent of my body weight! The MAG was a wonderful weapon, but it should only ever be carried by strong brutes who weigh well over 200 lbs. Those machine guns weren't only very heavy, you also had to carry 300 rounds of ammunition (in belts) plus the massive cleaning kit. You were even issued with a spare barrel, but no one ever took it with on patrol.

In the army my neighbour was "Sir," but we became equals the minute we removed our uniforms. I tried to reason with him, but in the end we had harsh words and ended our friendship. I also banned him from hunting on my property.

Sadly he was killed in action not long after and I got my FN back.

Being a crack shot is nothing to be proud of. Anyone who has good eyesight and steady hands can be a sniper. Shooting is just like golf, the more you do it the better you get at it. Not everyone, no matter how much they practice, will become a Tiger Woods though.

The first time I shot in the Rhodesian Service Championships I was naive enough to actually think I had a chance of winning. I knew I was up against the best sharpshooters in the country, but even in my wildest dreams I didn't expect one of them to be a "Tiger Woods."

We used Lee-Enfield .303's. To me those rifles were even more accurate than the more modern FN. If I remember correctly we started shooting from 200 yards, then 300, 400, 500 and eventually 600 yards. My score stayed within striking distance of the leaders until we reached the 600 yard mark. I could hardly see the target.

We each had 25 shots from that distance. You scored two points for a hit in the centre ring and one for a hit anywhere. I clearly remember scoring 13 out of 50 from that distance and I was more than happy with my score. It more or less meant I was capable of hitting a man-sized target from a distance of 600 yards with every fourth shot.

Then they announced Simon Rankin's score. I couldn't believe it, he had scored 49 out of 50! And to make matters worse, he wasn't happy with his score and demanded a recount!

I couldn't believe he could hit the centre of the target so many times from so far away. He couldn't believe that one of his shots wasn't in the centre!

A few years later I dropped a terrorist from a long way off, but there was no skill involved. It was sheer luck. He was running away from us and I only hit him with the seventh shot aiming well above his head. It was a hollow victory too because despite being wounded, the man managed to scramble to his feet and escape into the bush. Maybe I just nicked him?

We caught the woman who had been with him. We tracked her to a village and she was easy to identify because the urine had run down her dusty legs.

One of my friends told me an interesting story one day. He said that in Mashonaland a police reserve Land Rover patrol had come across a terrorist in a field. The man ran away. Then, when he was roughly 600 yards away and no doubt feeling safe, the terrorist stopped and looked back.

That was when Simon Rankin, who was standing on the back of the Land Rover, shot him right between the eyes.

Having seen him shoot on the range, I knew there was no luck involved.

What bad luck that terrorist had I thought. Had it been anyone else he would probably have been quite safe, but he stopped and looked back at a sniper who was probably capable of winning gold at the Olympic Games.

oooOooo

DYNAMITE COMES IN SMALL PARCELS

We were quite excited when we discovered the arms cache in the mountain on my farm. My pal Kobus saw a bit of olive green sticking out of a pile of leaves next to a massive granite boulder and called to Richard and me. Then the three of us set about scratching in those leaves. We dug out a couple of huge olive green canisters with Chinese writing and some numbers on them, but we didn't open them immediately. Instead we continued looking and then we found a black canister with English writing on it!

I recall the word "Heat" was written on that canister and when we read that we thought it was a heat-seeking missile. That was probably because not long before the terrorists had shot down a civilian passenger aircraft returning to Salisbury from Lake Kariba with a SAM-7 heat-seeking missile.

It turned out the canister held a 75 mm recoilless rifle shell though and so did those with the Chinese writing on them.

None of us had ever seen a live shell that size. If I remember correctly they stood almost two foot tall and we estimated that each weighed around 45 lbs.

It was late in the afternoon, the sun was setting fast and here we were on top of a massive rugged mountain. We held a quick conference to decide what to do next and when I think back about it now, the decision we made seems ridiculous.

We decided the army weren't going to get "our shells". Instead, we were going to make them into lamps for ourselves! In my mind I could see this beautiful lamp with its huge shiny brass casing standing in the corner of our lounge. I could also see my friends tugging fat wallets out of their pockets to buy similar lamps from me.

We packed the shells back into their canisters. The gooks had made bark handles attached to each canister for easy carrying. The three of us each slung a shell onto our backs and then hung a further shell on each shoulder. Then we headed for home.

The bush was so dense where we were that we couldn't walk upright, but had to duck under branches all the time. After walking about 25 yards all hunched up I gave up...

The weight was just too much. I decided the army could have my lamps after all and it didn't surprise me at all that both Kobus and Richard also swiftly gave up the lamp idea. We returned and hid the shells in a different place about 200 yards from where we had found them, and each of us carried a single shell down the mountain.

We suddenly emerged from the dense bush into a little open valley and knew immediately that this was where the gooks had been when the choppers had first attacked them. It was quite obvious because on the dense thorn bushes, surrounding the tiny clearing, hung hats and caps of all descriptions. Their headgear had been snagged by the thorns as the terrorists ran for their lives.

We also found a blood-soaked sock lying on top of a granite boulder with a trail of dried blood running down the rock.

I didn't say anything, but that sock had me thinking all the way down the mountain.

The morning after the battle with 200 terrorists on my farm three days before, I had helped find the bodies of the terrorists who had been killed. In fact, I had requested the Fire Force commander to drop the bodies next to my tobacco barns so my workers, who had been feeding them, would see them. As I explained to the commander, "If my men don't see the bodies they will think the gooks all got away and that Mugabe is winning the war".

He had intended to fly the corpses back to Grand Reef and then hand them over to the police for finger-printing and burial, but he readily agreed to my request because it made sense to him as well.

I clearly remember being amazed that all eight terrorists had been shot in the head. And not one had been shot in the foot so where did the sock fit in? I realised that a wounded terrorist had escaped.

The army had flown in two dog handlers with imported coon hounds to track down any wounded gooks. However, those dogs had proved to be quite hopeless despite their enormous potential to smell blood.

The two hounds had simply run from one body to another and never picked up a scent leading anywhere except to the next dead man and back again. One of the dogs had gone missing too, which rather upset his handler.

That dog arrived on our doorstep about a fortnight later looking rather sad. His ribs were sticking out and he was covered in engorged blue ticks. We dipped him to get rid of the ticks, fed him and returned him to the army.

It was almost dark by the time we arrived at my house and Kobus and Richard left for home immediately because it wasn't all that wise to drive around in Rhodesia after dark during those days. I plonked my giant shell down on the carpet in the lounge and the kids were quite amazed by its size.

Then I reported our find to the army on the radio and they told me they would come out to the farm at the crack of dawn the following day with a search party to see if we could find more weapons and ammunition.

They came at dawn and we searched Rutzenza mountain methodically and found an awful lot of stuff including a mortar. I managed to get the special branch man aside and told him about the sock and my suspicions. He told me that they would return that night and search my compound for the wounded terrorist.

Then they left with the entire "lamp factory stock" and late that afternoon one of my workers, Goodness, asked to speak to me. He looked quite forlorn. He told me that he had a terrific headache and could he please have some pain killers.

"Alarm bells" went off inside my head when he said, "pain killers". I had grown up with those people and understood them and their ways as well as any Rhodesian born farm boy would.

My workers often asked for medical help – Rhodesian farmers weren't just farmers. Of necessity they also had to be "doctors, midwives, funeral directors, veterinary surgeons, mechanics, counsellors, electricians, carpenters, advisors and money lenders". Asking for pills was not at all unusual, but asking specifically for "pain killers" was definitely very strange indeed.

Farm labourers always told you what their ailments were and then simply asked for *mashonga* which meant medicine. *Mashonga* also meant "magic" or more accurately "magic solution" and that is what they expected from both their boss and the local witch doctor whenever they became ill.

Whenever Boswell's Circus came to Umtali, I would take the workers for a rare treat. For days afterwards they would discuss what they had seen at the circus and anything they didn't understand would be explained with a "that man's got strong *mashonga*."

According to them the lion trainer, Eddie Fisher, who used to stick his head inside the lion's mouth had the most powerful magic of all. They may not have known much about trapeze artists, but they certainly knew what a lion was.

When Goodness asked for pain killers I had a brainwave. Trying hard not to smile, I said I had just the right thing, a brand new type of *mashonga* which was an outstanding pain killer. Eddie Fisher used the exact same *mashonga* whenever he stuck his head inside the *shumba's* mouth, I lied.

After telling him to wait by the workshop I went into the house where I soon located the bottle of what we called "brown pills." I can't remember the brand name, but I do recall they were the most vicious laxatives I had ever tried.

None of us ever had a brown pill, we always had half a brown pill because even a half would have you thinking your insides were being blown apart. After swallowing even that bit at night you only managed a few hours of peaceful sleep. After that you would drift in and out of sleep because your tummy would be growling and rumbling so much.

You also made sure you stayed near the bathroom the following morning until all the drama was history.

I filled Goodness's cupped hands with brown pills and sternly told him, "These are brilliant pills, but you must take them all at the same time otherwise they don't work at all."

"Yes Bwana," he answered and at that point I felt very guilty and wondered if I had done the right thing? What if he really had a headache? A handful of brown pills would probably get rid of his liver and spleen as well.

Then I watched him walk off and knew I had done the right thing. The pills weren't meant for him, they were for Mister Shot-in-the-Foot. I knew that because my workers, without fail, always went straight for the tap to drink their pills and Goodness had tossed the pills into his shirt pocket and was on his way back to his hut. I was quite confident the pills would be handed over to the wounded man as soon as possible.

Time would tell...

At 2 am, the police searched my compound for the wounded enemy and found nothing. I had wanted to go with, but they suggested I stay at home to guard my family. Afterwards the special branch man came to the house and told me they hadn't found anyone and I apologised for wasting their valuable time.

He just laughed and said, "No don't apologise, you did the right thing in letting us know and I still think you are right – there is a wounded terrorist around. He just isn't in your compound. We are going to search your neighbour's compound now and I'll let you know if we find anything."

The next day he phoned me and said they had captured the gook. He had been found in a hut on my neighbour's farm.

"You were spot-on," he said. "Half the guy's foot was missing. He probably got nailed by the chopper with the 20 mm cannon."

Then he said, "That guy was in such pain he shat everywhere. The blasted hut stank like a sewage farm. "

"My goodness," I said.

oooOooo

LAW UNTO THEMSELVES

Down in the Sabi Valley there lived a very unusual family, the Hicks. A father, mother and four sons. Before the war started no one took much notice of them, but they did talk about one odd thing they did.

The family did not allow policemen onto their land. Even more odd was the police accepted it. That is, until a young constable born and bred in Salisbury was stationed in the little village of Odzi.

One of his duties was to conduct a monthly motorcycle patrol to the farmers in the area. He planned his route on the map and then showed it to the Member-in-Charge for approval. The senior man took one look at it and then in horror said, "You can't go to the Hicks farm!"

"Why not?"

"They don't allow policemen on their land."

The new recruit was man enough to stand up to his superior. He told him in no uncertain terms, "We are the law, Sir. We can go anywhere and I'm going to visit the Hicks family on their farm."

The Member-in-Charge then called another policeman into his office to be a witness. He said, "Please yourself, but remember I have warned you that you are going to the Hicks farm at your own risk."

Through sheer coincidence old man Hicks was out hunting kudu that day and he happened to hear and then see the police motorcycle approaching. As the rookie crossed over the cattle grid onto his farm he fired a shot, which caused a puff of dust to erupt from the gravel road directly in front of the motorcycle.

The young cop whipped that big bike around in a flash and raced back over the grid and away from there as fast as he could.

After many years, and only after the war escalated, did the Hicks family allow the police back onto their land.

Rumour had it that the reason the family didn't like the police was because the Hicks family were dealing in illegal gold, but there was never any evidence of that.

The Hickses had a rough time during the war. Apart from several night attacks on their home, I recall two other incidents clearly because I was involved.

The first happened after we had cleared the road of landmines and were sitting drinking coffee on the veranda with old man Hicks. The one son had driven off to Umtali to deliver their milk and moments later we heard the sounds of battle. We immediately knew he had been ambushed. We grabbed our weapons and raced up the road, but when we got to the ambush the terrorists had disappeared.

The young man had driven through the ambush before stopping. He was lucky to be alive. His truck had several bullet holes and the front windscreen was shot to pieces. Although he hadn't been hit, a tiny splinter of glass had lodged in one eye. He lost the sight in that eye.

Another time on our way to the Hicks farm we came around a corner and saw old man Hicks' Peugeot truck lying on its roof. He had been blown up by a landmine not long before we arrived. He and his wife and small grandson had been on their way to Umtali to deliver a load of potatoes. One of his workers had been sitting on the back on top of the spuds.

His wife and grandson were standing next to the road and they were fine. Old man Hicks was still sitting upside down behind the steering wheel.

His one arm was trapped and he couldn't get out. We extricated him and found he had broken an elbow.

Sadly the worker was lying quite a distance away and he was dead. The entire road around the truck was covered in potatoes.

The Hickses weren't spared when the cattle rustling started. The first time some of their cattle were stolen, they reported it to the police which was perhaps unusual when you consider they'd banned the police from their farm.

The police tracked the rustlers for a long way before they lost the trail. Old man Hicks was furious and told the Member-in-Charge, "Next time I'll find my own cattle."

The Member-in-Charge gave him a stern warning not to take the law into his own hands, but old man Hicks retaliated with "You didn't find my cattle did you?"

Not long afterwards, they again stole some of the Hicks cattle. The old man and his four sons armed themselves, saddled their horses and set off to find the rustlers with the help of a Bushman tracker who worked for them as a shepherd.

Everyone knows that Bushmen are the best trackers in the world. They can read signs like a professor reads a book and this particular Bushman was no different.

On foot, he led the five horsemen right across that part of Manicaland, and into the Mrewa area of Mashonaland about 100 miles away and right to where their cattle were being held. Then the Hicks family took over and arrested the thief after giving him a good thrashing. Perhaps more than a good thrashing – they broke his jaw.

Apart from their own stock they also recognised the brands of other farmers in the Odzi area. They tied the thief behind a horse and then returned home with all the stolen cattle. After leaving their own cattle on their farm, they handed the other cattle and the thief over to the Odzi police.

It was a mistake on their part. Far from being grateful that someone else had done the police's work for them, the furious Member-in-Charge laid a charge against old man Hicks for taking the law into his own hands. They had also moved right through the middle of a "No go" military area in which the Selous Scouts were operating, the policeman said.

When the news filtered through the community, people were furious. Those who had lost many cattle to rustlers were the most angry.

Us farmers held a meeting at the Country Club and unanimously decided the Member-in-Charge had gone too far. People said he couldn't handle it that old man Hicks and his sons and the Bushman had succeeded where the police failed.

A four-man delegation was elected to go and speak to the Prime Minister, Ian Smith about it. The next day they drove up to Salisbury and later they reported back to us and said Smithy had intervened and all charges against the Hicks family had been dropped.

Rhodesia's leader was like that – a man who was always willing to listen to ordinary people.

oooOooo

MEETING

Gys Visser was a South African who moved to Rhodesia with his wife Ina. The farmers in our area were fairly conservative people who tended not to trust strangers until they knew them better. The Vissers soon proved to be ordinary nice folks and became very popular in the community. Ina was a school teacher with tremendous dedication and skill and everyone who met her spoke well of her.

The Odzi Country Club was our district's meeting place and one day the military invited all the farmers to a meeting there about security. I forget what rank the army man had, but he was high up, maybe a brigadier? He taped a map of Manicaland up on the wall and then started telling us what was happening where.

It was quite interesting and also refreshing to hear from the army in a public meeting for a change. The army generally tended to keep all things secret.

On his map the soldier had split Manicaland into several sections and he proceeded to tell us about terrorist numbers operating in each section.

"In this part of Maranke there are 300 terrorists at a time. They move in and out of Mozambique, but there are always about 300 of them. In the Honde Valley area there are 150 terrorists operating," he went on.

It was a very interesting talk, but also alarming because there seemed to be an awful lot of terrorists inside our country.

Then the military man invited questions.

Some men and some women asked questions, more it seemed to me, to appear to be important members of our community than anything else and then I saw Gys Visser's hand go up and I just knew he would ask a sensible question because unlike some of the others, he wasn't a pretentious person at all.

"Sir," Gys began. "I just want to ask ....the person who counted all these hundreds of terrorists in our province....why the hell didn't he shoot them?"

oooOoooo

AMBUSHED

Our task was a simple one. We had to escort a Pookie mine-detecting vehicle down to the Sabi Valley to clear the road so the only dairy farmer left in the valley could deliver his milk safely.

The Pookie was specially designed to find landmines. Its wide slick tyres were filled with helium, which enabled it to drive over a mine without setting it off. On each side of it hung a metal-detector wing. It had an armour-protected cockpit and bullet-proof glass windscreen to protect the driver.

The four of us in the escorting Kudu vehicle were farming neighbours and knew each other well. The Pookie driver, a cheerful young chap from Salisbury, introduced himself and told us he was rather nervous because it would be the first time he had gone into an operational area.

We told him not to worry at all. The trip down the Sabi road and back was nothing more than a milk run, we said.

Maybe he was more nervous than we thought because we had hardly left the village when the Pookie suddenly stopped in front of us with its rear warning lights flashing, the signal for us to stop immediately because the metal detectors had found something in the road.

We saw the cockpit hatch open and then the young chap emerged with a bayonet in his hand and started digging in the road. It didn't take him long to discover what the sensors had indicated. A car-flattened Coke tin buried in the gravel.

The same thing happened again at regular intervals and eventually we started getting mildly annoyed with the rookie driver ahead of us. We didn't tell him to ignore the warnings though. We knew he was merely doing his job and doing it well. We were just becoming impatient to get to the dairy farm where we knew a mug of coffee would be waiting for each of us.

Then when we were almost at the dairy farm we came around a corner and saw the Pookie had once again stopped with the lights flashing.

What we couldn't see was that a tree had been cut down and had fallen across the Pookie's path.

We watched the cockpit hatch being opened again and saw the driver's head and shoulders emerge. He faced us and shouted, "There's a tree lying across the road."

The next thing I heard was a shot.

That first bullet shattered the one warning light right next to the Pookie driver's hip and I saw him drop back down into the safety of the cockpit faster than a mongoose can evade a cobra after kissing the snake on the nose.

Then all hell broke loose as 20 terrorists opened up at us from point-blank range with a machine gun, automatic rifles and anti-tank grenades.

Without even thinking, the three of us in the back of the Kudu started firing furiously from behind the safety of the armour and bullet-proof glass. Of course we had to lift our rifles and heads over the top of the left hand side, but at least our bodies were protected.

What we weren't protected against were the anti-tank rifle grenades. They would burn through that armour plating in a flash and explode inside.

After emptying just one 20-round magazine, I grabbed the lever that released the grenades from their tubes on the sides of our vehicle. There was so much noise that we didn't hear them exploding. In fact, about half a minute later, Jan van Zyl started shouting at me to release the grenades and was quite surprised when I told him I'd already done so. I slammed another magazine onto my rifle and continue firing and then put in another and another until I found I had only one magazine left.

The two other blokes in the back with me were still firing when I grabbed the radio's handset and shouted, "Contact, contact." I gave our call sign and rough location over the radio and then I was rudely interrupted by the old man in our section, Chris le Roux.

He yelled at me, "Put the fucking radio down and shoot." His eyes were wild.

I didn't bother to tell him I was running out of ammunition.

I fired a few more shots and then noticed something very strange. Our driver, Herman Rogers, just sat there staring into space. It was quite amazing because of the terrific battle going on around him. What's more, I'd fired 120 rounds and my rifle was ejecting the hot empty cartridge cases straight onto his neck. Some of them had even rolled down inside his shirt.

Afterwards he showed us the blisters on his neck from the hot cartridge cases, but they couldn't have been that painful because he had just sat there without moving. He didn't try to reverse the vehicle or attempt to drive over our attackers and he didn't fire a shot either. He was totally traumatized by the suddenness of the attack.

I should have grabbed his ammunition, but it just never occurred to me.

Then the terrorists broke and ran. We opened the rear door of the Kudu and chased them. At that stage I didn't think about it, but later I found it very amusing that four guys had chased 20 terrorists. Herman had come out of his trance and joined us, but I don't think he fired a shot even then. The rest of us were all just about out of ammunition and resorted to firing rifle grenades at the fleeing enemy.

Afterwards an armed Lynx aircraft arrived above us, but although he circled the area for a long time the pilot never saw any of the terrorists.

We returned to the vehicles where we found the Pookie driver waiting for us. After lighting a cigarette, the best cigarette I'd ever smoked bar none, we examined the terrorist ambush.

We then worked out the number of terrorists that had lain in wait and that there had been 20 of them and that they had fired five anti-tank grenades at us. There were five separate bush fires burning on the other side of the road where those grenades had landed. We picked up 900 empty AK-47 and RPD machine-gun cartridge cases from that site.

Later we found out that we wounded one terrorist. That wound had become gangrenous, eventually killing him.

It had been one hell of a milk run.

oooOooo

TRAITOR

I had so much respect for the man. He seemed to be one of those quiet "pillars of strength" in the community. He was an elder in the church and I never saw him in the bar. If he ever went to the local pub I would surely have spotted him?

I saw him in church whenever I went. I would sit near the back and because he was one of the elders he sat on the side in the front facing us. He always seemed to be sleeping, but perhaps he was just "resting his eyes" like my granny always said whenever she nodded off.

He wasn't the sporting type and I can't recall ever seeing him at the club, but each to his own. He appeared to be a dedicated farmer and churchgoer. He was also much older than me so deserved my respect.

Now wise by hindsight, I know that during peacetime you can live in a community and never really get to know the majority of people well. You just think you know them and their ways. The only ones you really get to know are your close friends, and also those who cheat you when you do business with them.

One remembers the crooks and just tend to assume that everyone else is nice.

During a war, though, you get to see a man's true colours and what you see can astound you. The quiet-as-a-mouse little guy who hardly anyone ever notices may turn out to be a real hero when the bullets are flying and the big-mouth macho type often turns out to be yellow.

You discover other things as well.

Towards the late seventies some of us farmers near the Mozambique border suffered in many ways.

At our farm we took all the usual precautions and some others as well. We erected a high security fence around the house and filled the enclosure with seven dogs. One of them, a bull-terrier called Troubles, was rather ferocious. We also put up powerful security lights which shone outwards.

Thick wire mesh grenade screens were bolted across all the outside windows and there were plenty of these because our home was huge. Inside the main bedroom I packed sandbags to shooting height.

For some unexplained reason I was still in "it only ever happens to someone else" mode, but I did take one unusual precaution as well. I hid a home-made cannon among the flowers in the garden.

The cannon was just a thick steel pipe packed with explosive and sawed-up quarter-inch steel rod. The wires from it were buried up to just outside our bedroom window. From there they led up the wall and into the room, ending up attached to the firing box on my bedside table.

Each morning those wires were disconnected from the firing box: the tiny red warning light was likely to make the kids curious and children like to press buttons. Every evening, we would lock the security gates, let Troubles out of his cage, lock the doors and switch on the security lights.

Once the kids were in bed I would load my private arsenal of weapons and lay them out on a blanket on the floor behind the sandbags in our bedroom. Then I'd connect the cannon's wires to the control box.

I'd made careful plans as well. If we were ever attacked, I would first switch off all the lights in the house and then I would fire the cannon. After that I'd empty my army-issue FN at the attackers, lay it down and give them both barrels of my

Baikal 12-bore shotgun. It was loaded with triple-A buckshot.

Then they would get the seven rounds loaded into my favourite rifle, the Winchester 30-30. That would be followed by 32 rounds from the police-issue Sten gun and five rounds from the Brno .22. Then I'd empty my Colt .38 Special revolver.

After that it would be time to reload if they were still around. Reloading wouldn't take very long, it merely meant slapping another magazine onto my FN because I had a stack of loaded magazines ready. Loading the other weapons in the dark would take a bit longer.

The wife's duty was to inform the police by radio that we were under attack and then to attend to our four small children in an adjoining room. We knew it would take the cops about an hour to get to us so we only had to stay alive for that long.

I later discovered that plans and reality were two different things.

One night the wife and I sat watching TV. I'd cut out many a bullcalf testicle that day and was tired and so at exactly nine o' clock I told her I was going to bed. She asked if I would mind if she lay reading next to me while I slept? I had no objection, but then she remembered her book was in the car outside.

Of course I should have offered to fetch it for her, but for some lazy reason I said, "Well just go and get it."

She was scared to go out, but I managed to persuade her it would be quite safe and stood at the top of the high front steps while she fetched her book.

Twenty minutes later a gang of 12 terrorists attacked by firing a bazooka rocket at our bedroom window. Now almost 30 years later, my wife reminds me I had said it would be quite safe to fetch her book from the car outside.

Women are like that.

Being attacked was terrifying. Although the rocket missed our bedroom, it did manage to totally confuse us. I was just drifting off to sleep when suddenly my world went mad. I didn't have a clue what was happening. All I knew was that there was this rumbling noise inside my head. Then after my head cleared a bit I also heard the clatter of a machine gun and the crack of several AK-47s pounding out messages of death.

Perhaps my army training and my survival instinct took over. I will never know for sure.

I leaned over and pressed the cannon's firing button. That was one very powerful cannon and afterwards we knew it might have saved our lives. Through sheer luck it was pointed straight at the place under some msasa shrubs from where two terrorists had fired the bazooka.

The pieces of steel rod blasted a jagged hole through the security fence and shredded the leaves just above the terrorists. There was a good chance that some pieces of shrapnel had wounded them, but we never found any blood or other evidence of that.

They had another nine rockets laid out next to them and I seriously doubt we would have survived if they had fired them all at our bedroom window. Bullets do not go through thick walls, but a bazooka rocket is designed to penetrate a tank.

The rockets simply slice through bricks like a knife through butter. I'd seen them go through two walls and explode against a third.

The cannon's blast caused those two terrorists to leave in an awful hurry. So much so, they left their long line of rockets lying there. We found them the next morning.

After the awful deafening blast of the rocket and my cannon, the terrorists' rifle and machine-gun fire sounded like a bunch of popguns. I was happy to take them on, but I was hoping like hell they didn't fire another rocket at us.

I leapt out of bed and shouted to the wife to inform the cops by radio that we were being attacked. It was like talking to the trees. The little lady was in total shock and was crawling around on all fours in her nightie, so I grabbed the radio and told the police we were in deep trouble.

I think they said they would get there as quickly as they could. Words to that effect anyway.

Then I shouted to the wife to see to the children. That was when all her powerful mothering instincts came to the fore. She was into the kids' room in a flash and shoved them all in under a bed and then sneaked in there herself.

I grabbed the FN and started returning fire. I would fire a few shots from one window and then move to another and do the same from there while mother and children sang "Jesus loves me, yes I know" under the bed.

I kept moving from window to window, continually firing short bursts in the direction from where I heard the clatter of enemy fire. When my FN's magazine was empty, I didn't grab another weapon as I had planned, but simply slammed in another magazine.

And I didn't at any stage switch off the bedroom light. So much for plans.

The nightmare was soon over, though during the attack "soon" had seemed an eternity.

The next morning I saw I had caused more damage than our attackers. There was broken glass everywhere, kind courtesy of me shooting through windows. The police and I searched the area outside and judging by where we found empty shells and the rockets, we estimated that there had been a dozen terrorists.

I don't think we slept much the rest of that night, if at all, but when daylight arrived I suddenly became brave again. I had my own spies and informers and knew the terrorist gang leader's name was Garigayi. I also knew or rather suspected that my labourers were feeding him and his men.

So when the cook, Ernest, arrived for work that morning, I said to him, "Listen, you've been feeding Garigayi and his buddies so you know him well."

He didn't answer me, but I could see in his eyes that he was very surprised when I mentioned the terrorist gang leader's name. The police didn't even know that.

I continued, "I want you to give that idiot Garigayi this message: Tell him I say he and his men shoot like old women and tell him I sleep in the main bedroom not miles away over there (where the rocket penetrated another wall). Also tell him I'm going to kill him."

Not long after that, an army patrol clashed with Garigayi and seven of his gang. They killed six of the terrorists before the other two fled. They then followed a blood trail through the dense bush for miles before capturing a wounded terrorist. He told them the terrorist who had escaped was Garigayi.

He also said that Garigayi had been wounded in the head. His body was never found, but neither, to the best of my knowledge, did he ever attack anyone else again. He just disappeared off the face of the planet and my guess is he died from that head wound somewhere in the bush.

The day after we were attacked I sent my brave wife and the four little ones to live in town with their Granny while I stayed on the farm.

That night alone on the farm I wasn't so brave. In fact, I tossed a mattress on the floor in the passage just in case Garigayi decided to again try and fire a rocket into the bedroom. Even in the passage I couldn't sleep. Whenever one of the dogs barked at the moon I grabbed my rifle and ran to a window...

I wasn't attacked again, but my cattle started disappearing like money in the hands of a teenage girl. Week after week the rustlers would come at night and take small groups of cows.

They weren't real rustlers. I knew that. They were just ordinary peasants living in the Native Reserve who had no choice. The terrorists probably told them, "Go and steal that bastard's cattle or we will kill you and your family."

My life turned sour. Not only was I living apart from my family, but the massive herd of cattle we had built up over years was fast being eroded. Of course we tracked the rustlers each time cattle disappeared and cattle aren't difficult to track, but whenever we reached the Maranke Native Reserve we would lose the tracks because the locals had run their own cattle across the trail.

Sending my wife and small children away to a safer place was the only sensible thing to do as far as I was concerned, but two of my neighbours didn't think so.

They confronted me one day at the local rail siding while I was loading some steers for the abattoir before these were also stolen. They accused me of "taking the yellow route" because, as they put it, I had already sent my family packing and I had plans to leave as well.

Their wild accusations bemused me because they were two draft dodgers who had over the years avoided army duty like the plague. I reasoned that you shouldn't take draft dodgers too seriously.

They also told me firmly that if I was attacked they weren't going to come and help me. That coming from draft dodger neighbours who had heard on the radio we had been attacked and who stayed in their beds. Not that I expected anyone except the police and army to rush to my aid.

At that stage, I had no intention of going anywhere at all, but the attitude of those two did anger me and did perhaps play a small role into our eventual decision to quit farming and leave the country.

I tried everything to stop the rustling. I hung expensive bells around some of the cows' necks. I even hired a gunman, but it was all in vain.

It was an impossible task. My land was 4 760 acres in size and covered in mountains, kopjes and bush. There were 39 different cattle camps to watch and the most distant one was miles away.

One night two rustlers were killed in an ambush. The curfew law was the only advantage we had; no one was allowed to move around after dark. The hired gun and I thought that would put an end to the rustling, but the killings didn't help at all. About a week later another 50 cows were taken.

Eventually I had to terminate my gunman's employment because I could no longer afford him. My herd numbers had dropped far too low.

After that, security was just me and six dogs.

The seventh and most vicious dog, Troubles, had been fed meat with crushed glass in it. When the vet cut Troubles's stomach open he showed me the glass and how it had cut his stomach to ribbons and killed him. That scared me because I started wondering why they had killed the dog. Was it because they intended to come inside the security fence the next time they attacked?

Something else puzzled me.

I wasn't farming anywhere near a native reserve. There were several large farms between my land and the Maranke Native Reserve, yet my cattle were being stolen on a regular basis.

Some of the farmers bordering the reserve had also been attacked and had also had cattle stolen. At that time towards the end of the war, most of them had moved off their land and were struggling to make a living in town.

I could understand them leaving. After all, how could you make ends meet when your livestock is disappearing week after week? Besides, how do you live with yourself for the rest of your life if one of your children or your wife was killed in a terrorist attack or by driving over a landmine? I felt desperately sorry for those people and helped where I could.

There was still one man farming there, right next to Maranke, and throughout the war he had never been attacked and neither had any of his cattle been stolen. I couldn't understand that at all. The rustlers would walk across his land and also across several abandoned farms to mine where they would help themselves to my stock.

It didn't make sense. Why walk 30 miles in a night through a curfew area, risking your life, when you could just help yourself to cattle 500 yards away?

Then a friend told me something which explained everything.

He told me a black stranger had arrived on his farm one morning and asked to see him privately.

When they were alone, the stranger said the terrorists had sent him. They would not attack him or steal his cattle provided he paid them a certain sum of money each month until the end of the war.

My buddy was cunning and agreed to pay, but said unfortunately he didn't have any cash on the farm. The stranger willingly accepted a cheque from him.

The police were informed and they waited at the bank and arrested the man when he tried to cash that cheque. He was interrogated and spilt the beans. He told them only one farmer was paying the terrorists to leave him in peace, but that the plan had been to get others to do the same. It was his task, he explained, to recruit more farmers.

The man I had respected and who I never saw in the bar was the one paying the terrorists.

That traitor was the "straw" which broke the camel's back" in my case. I started making plans to leave Rhodesia.

oooOooo

ABOUT THE AUTHOR

The son of a tobacco farmer, Faan Martin, was born in 1947 in the scenic Rhodesian border city of Umtali. He was educated in Rhodesia and South Africa. During the war years he was a self-employed cattle rancher in the Manicaland province of Rhodesia.

The author did his national service with 1 Independent Company at the School of Infantry in Gwelo, in Wankie and at Sidindi Island on the Zambezi River border with Zambia. After completing his national service he served as a territorial soldier with the 4th Infantry Battalion starting as a rifleman and ending with the rank of sergeant. During his last six week stint with 4th Battalion, he served as Acting Platoon Commander.

He was awarded a General Service Medal and missed out on his long service medal by a few weeks. After almost 12 years in the army he was transferred to the Odzi Police Reserve.

During his time in uniform, he qualified as a marksman and served in the Operation Hurricane, Thrasher and Repulse areas. He also took part in external operations into neighbouring Mozambique and served with the Fire Force in Mashonaland. A Fire Force was a group of French Alouette helicopter gunships carrying troops who tried to react speedily to sightings or actual contacts with the enemy. Sometimes also to a murder or abduction provided the terrorists' trail was still fresh.

Martin fired at and was shot at by others including friendly forces, on nine different occasions. Once as a civilian.

In November 1978, Rhodesian Security Forces attacked 200 terrorists on a huge mountain on the Martins' 4 760 acre farm using helicopter gunships, a Lynx aircraft and Rhodesia Light Infantry troops. An attempt was also made to drop paratroopers, but on that particular day the wind was too strong for safe jumping.

Three days after the battle in which eight ZANLA insurgents were killed and a Rhodesian helicopter was shot down, the author and two friends searched the mountain and found a huge arms cache which included many 75 mm recoilless rifle shells – a heavy and quite vicious weapon which hadn't been used much by the terrorists up until that time.

Not long afterwards Rhodesian Special Branch policemen visited the author and his wife, Jayne, on their farm and warned them that their names had been found on a ZANLA death list after a highly successful attack on a massive terrorist base in Mozambique.

In January 1979, 12 terrorists launched a night attack on the Martins' farm house using a RPG-

4 rocket launcher, RPD machine gun and AK-47 assault rifles. The Martins survived the attack, but it changed their lives.

Concern over the safety of their four small children, the regular theft of their cattle, discovering that a neighbour was a traitor and knowing Robert Mugabe would soon become the new political leader of the country, eventually made the Martins decide to sell up and start a new life in South Africa.

After a short spell of teaching and farming in South Africa, Martin became a journalist. He has written 500 published magazine articles and was the Editor of two weekly newspapers, the *Northern Review* and *The Pietersburger.* Later he was the Assistant Editor of the *Farmer's Weekly* magazine.

He now lives in Scotland or put another way, near his granddaughter.

oooOooo

Lightning Source UK Ltd.
Milton Keynes UK
02 December 2009

146962UK00001B/15/A

9 781434 319739